Praise for *The Funny Life of Pets*

'I enjoyed eve___ of it. I think tha___ who reads it will laugh ___ off (much like I did). I r___ ___joyed the bit about begging and emotional blackmail. I hope that you will continue writing books.'

Emma, aged 10

'It's great. Very, very funny. Will there be another? I showed it to Ned and Thomas at school and they want a copy too.'

Arlo, aged 11

'Deliciously delightful. Superbly epic and funnier than any other book I've read.'

Ethan, aged 9

'I loved *The Funny Life of Pets*. It's funny AND sarcastic'

___oah, aged 9

For Daphne -
James Campbell

For my niece and nephew,
Olivia and Alfie x - Rob Jones

BLOOMSBURY CHILDREN'S BOOKS
Bloomsbury Publishing Plc
50 Bedford Square, London, WC1B 3DP, UK
BLOOMSBURY, BLOOMSBURY CHILDREN'S BOOKS and the Diana logo are trademarks
of Bloomsbury Publishing Plc
First published in Great Britain 2018 by Bloomsbury Publishing Plc
Text copyright © James Campbell, 2018
Illustrations copyright © Rob Jones, 2018

James Campbell and Rob Jones have asserted their right under the Copyright,
Designs and Patents Act, 1988, to be identified as Author and Illustrator of this work

A catalogue record for this book is available from the British Library

ISBN: PB: 978-1-4088-8994-7

4 6 8 10 9 7 5 3 (paperback)

Printed and bound in Great Britain by CPI (UK) Ltd, Croydon CR0 4YY

To find out more about our authors and books visit www.bloomsbury.com
and sign up for our newsletters

The author and publisher recommend enabling SafeSearch when using the Internet in conjunction with
this book. We can accept no responsibility for information published on the Internet.

THE FUNNY LIFE OF PETS

JAMES CAMPBELL

ROB JONES

BLOOMSBURY
CHILDREN'S BOOKS

LONDON OXFORD NEW YORK NEW DELHI SYDNEY

STOP!

Read this before you dare go any further . . .

◁ Fact ⚠ WARNING ⚠ WARNING ⚠ Fact ▷

Anything you think you might learn from this book might not be very accurate so should not be used in a school project or as part of your homework. Unless, of course, you are made of stardust and are as brave as sunshine.

WHAT SORT OF BOOK IS THIS?

> This is NOT a normal book.
> Not normal at all.

This is **not** a fact book as such. You won't find much practical information in here. If you're looking for **proper,** school-like stuff about pets then put this book down immediately and **run away screaming.** If it's practical information you really want, I can recommend the following books:

Boring Things about Pets
By Oswald Muesli

The Informative Guide to Having a Dog
By Lydia Dustbin

How to Look after A Goldfish
By Prof. Brian Yawn

This book is for four types of people:

1. People who have a pet and like reading about how **funny** they are.

2. People who don't have any pets but would really like one, two, three or **more.**

3. People who used to have a pet which has now 'gone somewhere else'. This book may stop you from feeling sad about it. Or make it worse.

4. People who don't have any pets, never had any, don't want any, don't care a rotten banana about them BUT like **laughing** and **giggling** until their head falls off and they turn into a donkey. Which is also a pet!

You don't read this book like a **normal book,** by starting on page 1 and then reading all the other pages in the **right order.**

BORING!

You can read this book forwards, backwards, sidewards and in approximately **861,000** different ways. On most pages you will find choices on **signposts.** To choose a path just turn to the page it says.

Some **choices** have signposts to tell you where to go next. Some pages have 'back' signposts, which tell you how to get back to where you came from. Sometimes there is **more than one** 'back' signpost because there is more than one way to get to the page that you're on. When this happens you can either **choose** to go back to where you actually came from or go back to somewhere you've never been before.

How often do you get to do that?

A warning about facts

Occasionally, this book will give you some actual facts.

> Cats are afraid of cucumbers. Go online and you will discover that the Internet agrees with this.

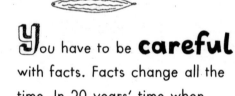

You have to be **careful** with facts. Facts change all the time. In 20 years' time when you give this book to your own children, half of the facts in this book will be **wrong.**

However, all of the *fictional* things in this book will still be true until the Moon gets **bored** and goes somewhere else.

Beginning page

Congratulations! You have arrived at the beginning of the book. **Decide** which chapter you would like to start with. Remember: there is no right or wrong **order** to read this book!

What are pets?

Let's start with the **basics.** What are pets? Well, I'm glad you asked.

Pets are **brilliant.** They come in different shapes and sizes. Some are **furry.** Some are **scaly.** Some are **so small** you can hold them in one hand. Others are twice the size of you and if they sit on you there is a danger you will **burst.**

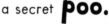

Some pets are **useful** and can fetch things, help people and even have jobs! Other pets just sit around all day doing nothing or, worse still, go behind your wardrobe and do a secret **poo.**

It wasn't me.

Getting a pet

We have now learned that pets exist. There's no denying it. We've all seen them. They are **real.**

So how do you go about getting one? Do you just **hope for the best** and maybe one day some sort of animal will turn up at the bottom of your bed?

What to do if you find a pet at the bottom of your bed: Page 61

This might work but it is quite **unlikely.** So how do you get one? How do you **convince** your grown-ups that you can have a pet? How do you decide which is the best pet for you to look after?

11

Emotional blackmail

Are you struggling to **persuade** your parents to get you the pet you want? Maybe they've come up with all sorts of **reasons** why you can't have one:

> We haven't got room.

> We haven't got time to look after it properly.

These are all just **excuses** (unless they are actually **real** reasons in which case you might have to settle for an imaginary pet).

Imaginary pets:
Page 224

Emotional blackmail is when you use your **imagination** to make them **feel bad** about not getting a pet. The sorts of things you might want to try are:

1. Draw a really **cute** picture of you and your family and include a picture of the pet you want. Then show the picture to your **grown-ups.**

Dad: What have you got there?

Child: I've drawn a picture. It's our family. That's me. That's you. That's mummy. That's Toby. That's Serena.

Dad: And who is this?

Child: That's Mr Fluffy-Wuff.

Dad: And who is Mr Fluffy-Wuff?

Child: He's the rabbit you are going to get me.

By Rob aged 28

Getting a Pet:
Page 11

2. **Y**ou can also try dropping it into **conversation** every now and again.

Ooh. This is a nice walk in the countryside. It would be much better though, if we had a dog.

I would really like to play Connect 4. If I had a pet to play it with me, I would play it all day long.

Playing Connect 4 with your pet:
Page 50

One pet bigger

If you are very lucky, your parents will be happy to get you a pet. One way to get the pet you want is not to ask for it at all but to ask for a pet which is bigger and more difficult to have in the house.

If you want a pet, you see,
Think of it as a **figure.**
Once that's done, just add
Plus one and ask for one pet
bigger.

If you want a **hamster**
To keep inside a cage,
Say you want a guinea pig
Of **any shape** or age.
'Oh no, no, no, you silly thing.
A guinea pig's too big,' they'll sing.
But if you use your biggest eyes
When parents use their head,
They'll come upon a **compromise**
And a hamster you will get instead.

Hamsters:
Page 138

But if you want a guinea pig,
What will you do now?
Well, say you want a catty puss
That purrs and goes **meow.**
'**Oh no,** what are you on about?
A cat is far too **big,'** they'll shout.
But if you use your **biggest** eyes
When parents use their head,
They'll come upon a compromise
And a guinea pig you'll get instead.

Guinea pigs:
Page 162

But if you really want a cat,
What will you do to **fix it?**
Well, say you want a floppy dog
To chew on bones and biscuits.
'Oh no, no, no, there is no room.
A dog is far **too big,'** they'll fume.
But if you use your biggest eyes
When parents use their head,
They'll come upon a **compromise**
And a cat you'll get instead.

Which-pet-
flow-chart:
Page 18

But if you **actually** want a dog
You need your common senses.
And say you want a pony horse
To ride and hurdle fences.
'A pony is **too big**, you brat.'
They'll say, 'We've only got a flat.'
But if you use your biggest eyes
When parents use their head,
They'll come upon a compromise
And a dog you'll get **instead.**

Dogs:
Page 69

But if you really want a horse,
You need to think **gigantic.**
You must request an elephant
To learn some **circus antics.**
'Oh no, oh heck, by Jove, by gumbo.'
They'll say, 'We have no room
for Jumbo.'
But if you use your **biggest eyes**
When parents use their head,
They'll come upon a compromise
And a **pony** you will get instead.

But if you want an elephant
The figures come unstuck.
Ask for an **Allosaurus**
But you won't have too much luck.
'Oh yes, yes, yes,' they'll surely say.
'A dinosaur is on its way.'
And 'cos you used your biggest eyes
And parents use their heads,
You'll **GET** a pet of Jurassic size
And it will eat **you** and your **bed.**

Begging

If all else fails, **begging** can be a very effective way
of getting your grown-ups to get you a pet. If you want a pet
you might have to get down on your knees and say, 'please,
please, please, please, please, please...
please can I have a pet? Please, please,
please...' etc.

Different types
of horse:
Page 20

Which-pet-flow-chart

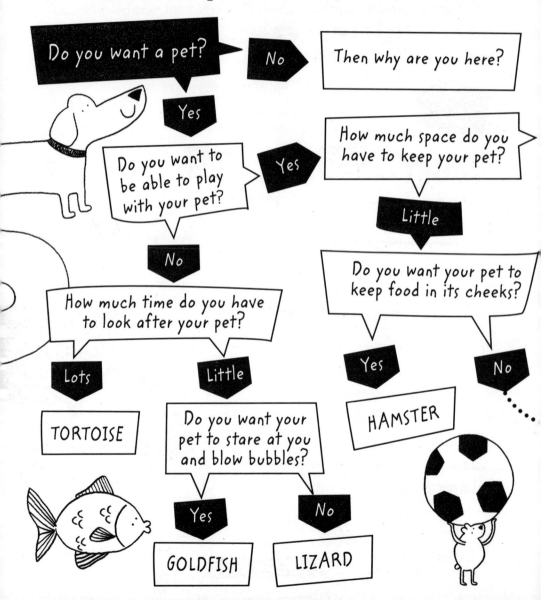

If you can't **decide** which pet to get, simply use this flow chart. Start at the beginning and **follow** the chart until you get to a pet.

Lots

Do you want your pet to lick your face and hide your slippers?

No

Yes

DOG

Do you want your pet to be obsessed with balls of wool?

Yes

No

CAT

HORSE

Do you want to read about your pet on a Peruvian restaurant menu?

No

IMAGINARY PET

Yes

GUINEA PIG

Different types of horse

To some people, one horse looks like any other horse but there are in fact many **different** types of horse. If you want to know all the different breeds of horse, get a book on horses or go online. Here, however, are some of my **favourite** ones.

SUFFOLK PUNCH

These are known as **gentle giants** but I wouldn't want one standing on my foot, I can tell you. These aren't really for riding. They are better at pulling massive trailers and jumbo jets. They would make a great pet if you want your pet to do a **poo** the size of your head.

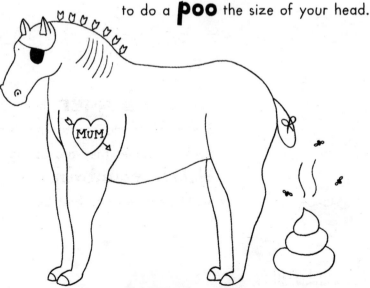

SHETLAND PONY

These are **extremely small** ponies but you can still ride them. (Although you will get too big to ride it quite quickly and will need to get a proper horse.) I like their **cute fringes** and the fact that when there is a full moon they glow a yellowy-green colour.

WELSH MOUNTAIN PONY

These are **bigger** than Shetlands. In fact, according to my book on ponies they are as big as a **Welsh mountain.** Although I might have misread that bit.

Feeding a pet

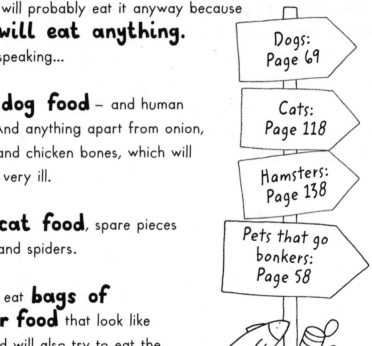

It is very **important** to feed pets the right thing. If you try and give dog food to a hamster it will not be very happy and if you try and give hamster food to a dog... the dog will probably eat it anyway because **dogs will eat anything.** Generally speaking...

Dogs eat **dog food** – and human leftovers. And anything apart from onion, chocolate and chicken bones, which will make them very ill.

Cats eat **cat food**, spare pieces of cheese and spiders.

Hamsters eat **bags of hamster food** that look like granola and will also try to eat the fingers of small children.

Dogs:
Page 69

Cats:
Page 118

Hamsters:
Page 138

Pets that go bonkers:
Page 58

Guinea pigs eat almost the **same thing** as hamsters but you can buy a slightly bigger bag as they will live longer.

Goldfish eat **fish food** – be very careful not to give them too much or they will eat it all, get extremely fat very quickly and then **explode** and cause a mini tsunami in your fish tank which will **destroy** all your house plants and cause **dinosaurs** to evolve from your carpets.

Ponies eat the **grass** that's in their field and hay in the winter. They are also very fond of carrots and a **sugar lump** or two.

Guinea pigs: Page 162

Goldfish: Page 196

Ponies: Page 178

Equipment for feeding your pets: Page 24

Famous pets throughout history: Page 132

Equipment for feeding your pets

Unless your pet is a wild animal and will find food for itself, you are going to need some **equipment and food** to feed it with. Obviously, the stuff you're going to need will depend on the pet you have.

Below I have **mixed up** the food with the pet. See if you can sort it out.

It is really important to get the **right food** for the right pet. Unless, of course, your pet is an imaginary pet. If you get yourself a **Norfolk lemur,** for example, you can feed it cupcakes, used nappies and daffodils. It'll be very happy with any of those.

Impossible imaginary pets: Page 227

Feeding a pet: page 22

Royal Society For Made-Up Animals: Page 174

Getting a rescue pet

You don't have to get a brand new pet: sometimes it is better to get one **second hand.**

Pet rescue centres are places where **wonderful people** look after stray pets, pets that have been found and pets whose owners can't look after them any more for **whatever** reason.

Getting a rescue pet does not necessarily mean getting a pet that is able to **rescue people** in distress — but it might do. All around the world there are police dogs and fire service dogs who help rescue people from collapsed buildings and **blizzards!**

Getting a pet:
Page 11

Pets that can
do jobs:
Page 172

How to use your imagination

How often do people tell you to use your imagination?

> Dad, why haven't I got any dinner on my plate?

> I haven't cooked anything. You'll just have to use your imagination.

Has anyone ever told you **HOW** to use your imagination? There are **millions** of ways to do it but I'll tell you just one...

Find somewhere **quiet** and sit still with your eyes closed. Make sure that you are calm and your breathing is **calm** too. Then ask yourself inside your head, 'What am I going to think about **next?'** And **finally,** listen to your head or watch the inside of your brain or pay attention to yourself and see what you think of next.

You'll probably be quite surprised at what is going on in your imagination. Try it every day for a month and you'll get quite good at it.

Pet toilet behaviour

Humans do it in toilets but how do pets do it? Well, it depends what type of pet you have. Goldfish tend to do their **poos** as they swim along which is a **bit weird.** If you did that in your local swimming pool you'd get in a lot of trouble. I certainly did.

Go online and look up 'cat poo toilet' and you'll find that cats might go for a poo on your toilet from time to time!

Lamp posts: Page 30

Toilet training: Page 32

Poo identification table: Page 34

LITTER TRAYS

If you have a cat you will probably need a **litter tray.** This is a rectangular tray full of weird stuff called litter. Cat litter is not stuff thrown away by cats.

The cat litter absorbs moisture and some of the smell, so that the **cat's wee** disappears and its poos dry up into strange super hard poos (which should definitely not be used as weapons or golf balls).

A funny story about litter trays: Page 194

Once you have got your cat or kitten, you will spend a lot of time watching it and waiting for it to look like it is about to do a wee or a poo. (It will probably start looking for a corner, have a **strange expression** on its face and might cross its legs.) As soon as you notice any signs of toilet behaviour, pick it up and plonk it in the litter tray. The cat should then get the message that this is where you want it to do its business.

By the way, cat litter is called cat litter because 'poo-gravel' is rude.

LAMP POSTS

If you get a dog, **lamp posts** will suddenly become much more important to you. You'll notice that your dog is incredibly interested in lamp posts, trees, fence posts and bollards. This is because dogs **love weeing** on them. I don't know why they do this. I think it's because they use their wee to send **messages** to each other.

As far as I can tell though, the only message they seem to be leaving says:

I have done a wee here!

I don't think they are sending each other **important messages** like:

Be careful around here. Cars come round that corner really quickly so make sure you're on your lead.

Dogs: Page 69

Ponies: Page 178

Pet toilet behaviour: Page 28

No. As far as I can tell, when a dog is sniffing a lamp post, this is what he is thinking:

Ooh. This is interesting. A spaniel did a wee here three days ago. That spaniel usually wees on that bush. Maybe I'll have a sniff of that bush and see what's going on. Ooh the spaniel has not weed on this bush but a poodle has. I recognise this poodle. It's Oscar from number 43. And he had sausages for his dinner last night. And what is this smell? Oh my goodness, this is the smell of **my** wee. I must have done a wee here a month ago and I had completely forgotten about it. Thanks to my amazing sense of smell I can discover places I have weed and forgotten about.

If you like the sound of this sort of thing, you should probably get **a dog.**

If you don't, maybe you should take a look at **ponies.** If a pony did a wee on a lamp post the force of the wee would probably knock it over. And anyone walking past.

NEWS
RUFF TIMES
AHEAD FOR
DOGS.

DAILY
HOUND

ADVERT

DOG LOSES
HAT

Toilet training

The only pets that can be **toilet trained** are cats and dogs. Goldfish poo wherever they want. Guinea pigs and hamsters seem to poo wherever they are. Ponies are unpredictable with their pooing and, when they do them, the consequences are enormous.

If you are trying to train your puppy then you need a **garden.** You then need to spend **hours** of your life walking your puppy around the garden having conversations with it like this:

YOU: Why do you think we are in the garden?

PUPPY: I love you.

YOU: Yes, that's lovely but why do you think we are in the garden — in the rain?

PUPPY: I love you.

YOU: I know, but that's not important right now. Why are we in the garden, in the rain, getting wet?

PUPPY: I don't know. I only know that I love you.

Litter trays: Page 28

YOU: We are in the garden getting wet so that you can do a poo!

PUPPY: Oh.

YOU: Why won't you do a poo?

PUPPY: I'm waiting until we go back in the house. Then I will do my poo on the sofa.

Poo identification table

Here is a **handy table** to help you identify an **unexplained poo** you might find. This table will also help you decide whether you can cope with the poo of a pet you might fancy having. For example, if you think you might like a rabbit, check out its poo **first.** Could you handle having that **on your hands?**

Cat poo:	Dog poo:
Cat poos are weird bullet type things that are sometimes hairy. They smell quite horrible.	The smelliest, stickiest poo in the world. You need special bags to pick it up with, special bins to put it in and if you leave it lying in the street people get very cross indeed.
Lizard poo:	**Goldfish poo:**
Good news: Lizard poo smells like hot chocolate. Bad news: It doesn't really. 	Sometimes they hang out of the goldfish's bum for ages. Don't believe me? Look up 'long goldfish poo' on the Internet!

Hamster poo:

Good news: Hamsters only poo when they are frightened.

Bad news: Hamsters are frightened all the time.

Rabbit poo:

Rabbits often eat their own poo (search online for 'bunnies eating poo' and you'll find SO. MANY. VIDEOS.), which is why I don't mention them much in this book.

Pony poo:

Gigantic poos. Imagine your head, but made out of poo. That's how big a pony's poo is. For some reason though, you can leave them on the road and no one minds!

Imaginary poo from an imaginary pet:

These can vary enormously. They can smell of roses and sparkle with fairy dust, or they can be huge and smelly and run around and get completely out of control.

ONLY ONE IMAGINARY POO ALLOWED IN SHOP AT ANY TIME.

Pets that aren't in this book much: Page 236

A funny story about litter trays: Page 194

How to prove you know how to look after a fish: Page 204

Playing with pets

One of the **best things** about having a pet is that you can play with it. In fact, most pets will let you play with them all day and never get tired. (With the possible **exception** of cats – who will let you play with them for as long as they want and then they will **attack you!** Look up 'moody cat alert' and see for yourself!)

There are **many games** you can play with pets. These include fetch, chase, hurdling, tummy tickling, hitting it on the head with a sausage, racing and **Connect 4.** To make things **complicated** I have created a chart which shows you which games are suitable for which pet.

Most pets can't see the difference between playing, working and just being a pet. To a **happy pet,** everything is **play.** This means that they are often easy to train to do certain things.

Pets that go bonkers: Page 58

Which pet is the best to play with?: Page 45

Holidays on the Moon: Page 148

Game-pet chart: Page 48

36

What you can teach your pets to do

Dogs are the **easiest** of pets to teach. You might want to start with a clicker and some treats. A **clicker** is a clicky thing you can get from a pet shop. It makes a click sound that your dog can hear really clearly. As you train your dog, it will learn that this click is really important and it should pay attention. Treats are small bits of food, **not trips** to theme parks.

Roll over and I'll take you to Legoland.

Go online and look for videos on training dogs. You can train them to sit, do things with their paws and even run small businesses.

Most dogs love to **fetch.** Sticks and balls are the most popular, although some dogs will also fetch slippers, newspapers and **weird furry things** that live in the gap between the bin and the dishwasher. Sometimes, dogs just can't fetch though. Have a look at some of the **'Dog Fetch Fails'** videos on YouTube.

Playing fetch with your dog: Page 44

Cats like to learn stuff but you can only teach them simple things like **robbing banks** and taking over the world by stealing nuclear missiles.

Guinea pigs can be **taught** to come to you when you call their name (search for *'How to Teach a Guinea Pig to Come when Called'*). And fish can be trained to **follow your nose** if you put your face against the glass.

Some pets are **so clever** that you can even train them to do actual jobs...

Pets that can do jobs: Page 172

Tickling the tummies of hamsters and guinea pigs

Hamsters and guinea pigs spend most of their life being **terrified** and one of the best ways of making them feel safe is to handle them, talk to them and gently **tickle** their tummies.

Use just your **fingertips.** You don't need any sort of equipment to tickle a hamster. In fact, you **MUST NOT** use any equipment to tickle a hamster. If you need extra help, look for **'Ticklish Guinea Pig'** on YouTube. You'll get to see it stick its feet in the air!

> Where are you going with that ladder?

> I'm just going to tickle the hamster.

Hamsters and guinea pigs **love** having their **tummies tickled** but it is possible to over-tickle the little furry ones. You will know if you have overly tickled a guinea pig because its face will go **red** and a **little bit of wee** will come out of its bottom end.

Safe and ethical experiments you can do with your pets

Lots of people think that doing experiments on animals is **wrong.** Here are some experiments and tests you can do with your pets that definitely **won't hurt** them and they might even enjoy:

Cats in a Circle

I recently discovered an **experiment** to see if cats will sit in a circle. Draw or tape a circle on the ground and most of the time, your cat will want to sit in the middle of it. Check out the **3,879 videos** on YouTube: Search for **'Cats Can't Resist Sitting in Circles.'**

I have tried this. I drew a circle in the middle of my kitchen floor. I discovered that a cat will only sit in the middle of this circle if you **own a cat**. Which I don't.

CAT GOES HERE

PERMANENT

Does Your Dog Love You?

1 What does it do after you have fed it? This shows you its **top priority** after food. Does it want to play by itself or does it want to **cuddle** you?

2 What happens when you leave it **alone** at home? Does it **freak out?** If it does, this doesn't mean it loves you. It means it is very **anxious** about being left alone. If your dog happily goes to its bed when you're out, then it knows you are coming home and feels **safe.**

3 What does your dog do when you get home? Does it make a **fuss** of you, wag its tail and lick your face? Then it loves you. If it doesn't even get off the sofa then it's **not that bothered.**

4 Does your dog give you a **card** on St Valentine's Day?

Even the **Wall Street Journal** thinks there's a way to **test** how much your dog really loves you. Search for 'Five Ways To Know Your Dog Loves You' on YouTube.

Which pet breathes more?

Get yourself a stopwatch, a piece of paper and a pen. Watch how often your pets **breathe.** If it's a hamster you'll see that its tummy goes in and out. If it's a goldfish you will see that its gills go in and out. Count how many times your pet breathes in a minute. Then **time** some of your other pets, or other people's pets. Then time yourself and your grown-ups.

How many times do we breathe in a minute?

Make a table of the **results**. Which pets breathe the **most** and which the **least?** The only problem with this is that you might get so **excited** you **forget** to breathe!

ALWAYS REMEMBER TO BREATHE!

Do your pets have a favourite colour?

Try getting **different** coloured food bowls for your pets. Offer them some food in a **blue** bowl and some food in a **red** bowl. Which bowl do they prefer? Maybe it's their **favourite** colour. Maybe it doesn't make any difference. What an **interesting** experiment.

Write down the results and then email me at: iamnotreallythatinterested@whatever.com

Guinea pigs: Page 162

Getting a kitten: Page 125

Are cats afraid of cucumbers?: Page 66

Made-up types of cat: Page 216

Playing fetch with your dog

The way to teach a dog to **fetch** is to throw something for it. A **ball** is good for this. Some dogs will bring it back to you while other dogs will just stare at the ball in confusion and then ignore it. It depends what sort of dog you have.

Retrievers fetch balls.

Terriers destroy balls. Look up *'Terrier Destroys Ball'* and see one in action for yourself!

Collies and sheepdogs gather balls together in groups.

Chihuahuas stay where they are and shout at balls.

Pomeranians decorate balls and display them for the admiration of their friends.

Spaniels get half way to the ball and then forget what it is they are doing and wander off to the shops.

After a while of teaching your dog to fetch things you will feel quite **pleased** with yourself until you realise that what has actually happened is that your dog has taught **you** to throw things for him.

44

Which pet is the best to play with?

I asked **100 school children** to choose which pet they thought would be **best** to play with. Here are the results:

Dogs: 32%
Cats: 24%
Ponies: 10%
Guinea pigs: 18%
Hamsters: 14%
Fish: 2%

I also asked **100 guinea pigs** who they would be like to be played with by. Here are the results:

Children: 79%
Grown-ups: 12%
Other guinea pigs: 6%
Cats: 1%
The Toronto Maple Leaf ice hockey team: 2%

Things that shouldn't be in this book: Page 239

Playing with pets: Page 36

Pet racing

There are three main types of **pet racing.** They all involve seeing how fast your pets can get from one place to another. The **three types** of pet racing are:

1. Racing one pet against another pet

of the same type. For example: seeing which of your two guinea pigs can get to the end of the dining room table first. Google *'guinea pig race'* and you'll see some top athelete guinea pigs racing against each other!

2. Racing pets against other pets of

different types. For example, which is faster — cats or dogs?

3. Racing pets against yourself. For example,

can you get home before your cat does?

Obviously racing a goldfish against a pony isn't very **fair.** You can get vehicles for pets which could even out the odds, a bit.

If you want to know **which pets** you could race against each other, here is a diagram to show you the **top speeds** of various pets:

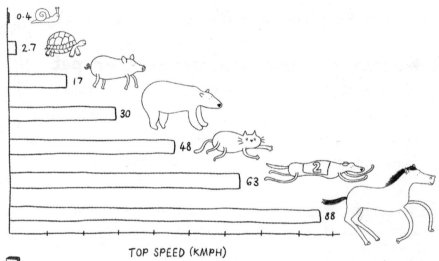

0.4
2.7
17
30
48
63
88

TOP SPEED (KMPH)

Even though cats are only the third-fastest pet in this diagram, they often have a **mad half hour** in the evening when they run around the house leaping from one piece of furniture to another. During this period they are actually the **fastest** animals in the universe and can travel fast enough to leave the orbit of a small moon. Look up **'The 41 Most Unexpected Cat Jumps of All Time'** on YouTube.

Game-pet chart: Page 48

Game-pet chart

	DOGS	CATS	HAMSTER
FETCH	✔ Playing fetch with your dog: Page 44	✘	✘
CHASE	✔	✔ Playing chase: Page 52	✘
TUMMY-TICKLING	✔ Tummy tickling: Page 79	✔ But don't say I didn't warn you	✔ Tickling the tummies of hamsters and guinea pigs: Page 39
SAUSAGE BOPPING	✔ Bopping dogs on the head with sausages: Page 100	✘	✘
RACING	✔	✘	✘
CONNECT 4	✔	✔	✔ You could have an amazing winning streak!

If you don't know how to play with your pet, this is the chart for you! It will also help you remember to never tickle a pony's tummy or race your imaginary pet.

Playing with pets: Page 36

Imaginary Pets: Page 224

GUINEA PIGS	PONIES	FISH	IMAGINARY PET
✗	✗	✗	✓ Only if you like fetching for yourself!
✗	✗	✗	✗ You have to be really good at acting!
✓	✗	✗ You might get wet hands though	✗
✗	✓	✗	✓
✗	✓	✓	✓
✓	✓	✓	✓

Sausage-horsing: Page 188

Pet racing: Page 46

Playing Connect 4 with your pet: Page 50

Playing Connect 4 with your pet

Connect 4 is one of my **favourite** games. It's really easy to learn but extremely hard to play well. The way to **win,** of course, is to play against an animal! Look up *'Amazing* **Dog Trick** *– Kooikerhondje Cleo Plays 'Connect Four''.* The only different **rule** you need to know is that if your opponent doesn't make a move after one minute, it has to miss a turn and you get to go again.

Let me give you an example. Yesterday, I played Connect 4 against my friend's hamster. The hamster is called **The Duke of Smellington.** I was red, the hamster was yellow. I went first and put one of my red pieces in **slot 4.**

Brilliant names for all sorts of pets: Page 130

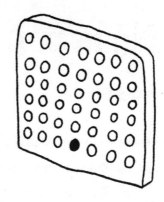

I gave the hamster a **full minute** to put one of his yellow pieces in a slot but he didn't so I got to place another piece. I put it in slot 4 again.

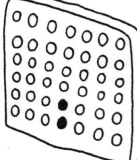

Again, the hamster didn't move so I moved again. And despite the fact that I was clearly about to win, the Duke of Smellington didn't move at all. He just **stared at me.**

And so I **won.**

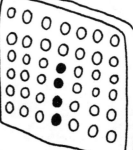

Game-pet chart: Page 48

Record-breaking pets: Page 211

51

Playing chase

Playing **chase** with your pet is quite similar to pet racing but it's not necessarily the fastest pet that will win.

Dogs are not as **fast as horses,** but horses usually can't be bothered to chase people. Dogs love playing chase and will do it all day.

Cats will chase you if you have something they want and when they catch you they will usually scratch you or call you a rude word in **cat language.** Look up 'Cat Attacks Man and Chases Him Down' online and see for yourself.

How rude!

MEOW!

Hamsters will chase you if you **glue** sunflower seeds to your feet and encourage them with whistled tunes.

Fish will only chase you if you are in the tank **with them.** That would need to be a pretty big tank.

I once chased a wasp around my kitchen until the wasp realised that it was much more **scary** than me, then the wasp chased me around the kitchen until I hid in a cupboard. But it wasn't a pet wasp so I don't know why that story is even in this book.

Things that shouldn't be in this book: Page 239

Game-pet chart: Page 48

Trouble with pets

Owning a pet is great but sometimes they can break things, get poorly or do **weird stuff** that makes you think, 'Why is he doing this?' or 'What am I going to do about that?'

I could write a whole book about pets **causing trouble.** Here are just few things that might happen to your pet that you'll need to deal with.

Beginning Page: Page 9

My dog has worms:
Page 64

My pet is sick:
Page 68

Life expectancy of hamsters:
Page 144

Why have I got so many hamsters?:
Page 146

1. My dog has got worms – in its bum!

2. My pet is poorly and I don't know what to do!

3. My hamsters keep dying!

4. Why have I got so many hamsters?

5. It turns out that someone in my house is allergic to my pet!

Someone in your house is allergic to your pet:
Page 235

Complications caused by keeping animals in the bath

Let's say that you **really want** a pony but you don't have a field or a stable to keep it in. Can you simply put the pony in your **bath?** Or imagine you have too many hamsters. The man in the shop told you they were both girls but somehow they have made **loads** of baby hamsters who are all making families together and now you have about **300** hamsters and don't know what to do with them. Can you simply put them in your bath?

Why have I got so many hamsters?: Page 146

Or maybe you've read a copy of *Impractical Fish Keeping* and have decided to **adopt a killer whale.** Can you keep one in your bath?

Well, you can, but there will be **consequences.**

The **main problem** is that you won't be able to have a bath.

Can I have a bath?

No.

Why not?

The bath is full of animals.

RACING POST

The other problem will be that your pet will probably get **really bored** being in the bath all day. You would have to get a television for it or something.

Famous pets throughout history: Page 132

Ponies: Page 178

Circumstances change making it impossible to keep your pet: Page 234

Pets that go bonkers

Every now and again your pet will go **bonkers.** This is usually because you've done something you shouldn't have. So here are some things you shouldn't do and some things you should **watch out** for:

Dogs

Be careful around the teeth area. Those teeth are **sharp** and sometimes if a dog gets too excited they can snap. When you're playing with your dog, if it starts growling, the play has got **too rough.** If you want to see all kinds of dogs going bonkers, take a look at *'Funny Angry Dogs Barking And Growling Compilation'* videos on YouTube.

Never bother a dog when it's eating. In fact, **never** bother anyone while they are eating. Get on with your **own dinner!**

Cats

Cats are unpredictable **little gremlins** at the best of times. Things to watch out for include a wagging tail and growling.

If your cat does that, run like heck and hide in a cupboard until the authorities have arrived. Check out some of the *'angry cat videos compilations'* on YouTube.

Being attacked by cats: why have you got scratches on your face?: Page 156

Hamsters

Generally speaking, the only thing a hamster will attack is a sunflower seed, but if you are unlucky enough to get a **bad-tempered** hamster, you'll find that dressing up as a bird of prey and swooping around the utility room should make it run back into its little house. Hamsters can **growl** though. Search for *'angry hamster'* online.

Guinea pigs

Guinea pigs do occasionally go bonkers. You'll know they are about to get **dangerous** when they start making a noise like a **kettle** and go bright purple. If this happens, drop, roll and cover, then go on holiday immediately. To the Moon.

Holidays on the Moon: Page 148

Fish

The **only way** you can be attacked by a fish is if you are in the water with it. If you are in the water with a fish and it attacks you, simply get out of the water and go and have a **shower.**

Ponies

There are **lots of rules** you must follow when around horses. One thing is for sure: don't **creep up** on horses from behind. They hate that. And for some reason, you have to get on a horse from the left side. If you try and mount a horse from the right side it will start **giggling** and fall over. If you want to see a horse going bonkers look up *'horse going crazy in field'* and you'll see a bunch of ponies and horses go mad!

Lions

If you have a **pet lion** then you will need one thing. A new brain! Why would you have a pet lion? If you are silly enough to get a pet lion then you deserve everything you get. And what you'll get is **eaten.**

Feeding a pet: Page 22

Playing with pets: Page 36

What to do if you find a pet at the bottom of your bed

You **never know** what's going on when you're **asleep.** Every now and again you will wake up to find some sort of animal at the end of your bed. The first thing you need to ask yourself when this happens is this:

> *Does this animal belong in my house?*

If the animal is your dog, for example, waking up to find him in your **bedroom** is very exciting. He will probably jump onto your bed and **lick your face** until you cry.

If the animal is someone else's pet or a wild animal, this is a **different matter.**

Wild animals that you don't want turning up at the end of your bed include **wasps** and **polar bears.** The worst animal to find at the end of your bed is **a wasp with a pet polar bear.**

If a dangerous animal such as this appears in your bedroom, your best bet is to **hide** under the duvet and be **very, very quiet** until they go away. There is no point trying to run away because polar bears can run at 30 kilometres per hour so you can't outrun it. The thing to do is call for a grown-up. It doesn't really matter if they are a **responsible** grown-up or not. Any grown-up will do.

> Definitely don't try to feed the polar bear like the people in 'A Polar Bear Came to Visit' did. Look it up online to see what happened!

When the grown-up is with you in the room, that is the time to **run away.** The grown-up will run away too. Now you don't have to be **faster** than the polar bear — you just have to be faster than the grown-up!

Some people find it best to keep a polar bear **repellent machine** in their bedroom. You can get one from Bucheto.

Getting a pet:
Page 11

Machines from
Bucheto:
Page 190

My dog has worms

What? Your dog has **worms?** Where? Worms live in the garden, surely? Yes. Worms do live in the garden, but there is a **certain type** of worm that lives inside dogs and other animals.

For some reason, when dogs are out in the woods and places, they occasionally **eat poo.** I know that's disgusting but it's just part of the wonderful weirdness that is dogs.

Sometimes the poo has **worm eggs** in it. Worms don't do a huge amount of **damage** to dogs but you want to **get rid** of them fairly quickly. You can get worming tablets from the vets. They aren't very expensive and they get rid of the worms.

I love poo.

Poo Identification Table: Page 34

The vets: Page 225

Or you can use an **old trick** where you sing songs to your dog's **bum**. This song has been written to encourage all the worms to come out and play.

These are the words of the song:

Wormy wormy
Please come out and play
Wormy wormy
Come and play with us today.
Wormy wormy
Wriggle through the bummy door
Wormy wormy
Come and play Connect 4.

Trouble with pets: Page 54

Dogs rubbing their bums along the ground: Page 104

How to test if a grown-up is responsible: Page 198

When the worms come out, don't play Connect 4 with them. Just **scream** for a responsible adult.

Are cats afraid of cucumbers?

If you go online and search for 'cats afraid of cucumbers' you will find all sorts of **hilarious** videos of cats being **terrified** of cucumbers.

I spent **three hours** watching these videos and generally, this is what happens: a cat is eating its dinner and then its owner quietly places a cucumber behind it or to the side. Then we wait... the cat finishes eating... turns around... sees the cucumber and **BOING!** The cat leaps up in the air in a startled fashion and then runs away hissing.

It definitely looks like the cat is afraid of the cucumber, but I'm **not convinced.** I think the cat is just surprised by the cucumber and would be just as surprised if you put anything **unexpected** next to it while it was distracted.

If you have a cat, maybe you should do some **experiments** and see what things make the cat jump.

Safe and ethical experiments you can do with your pet: Page 40

I tried this on my **friend's cat** and found that it was afraid of cucumbers, courgettes, a bottle of fizzy drink, 27 toy soldiers, a cheese plant and an alarm clock. But it was not afraid of a photograph of **Horatio Nelson,** a pack of sausages, a banana and a stuffed toy owl with sparkly eyes.

Getting a kitten: Page 125

Ten things you didn't know about cats: Page 131

My pet is sick

Unfortunately, every now and again, pets do **get sick.**
When this happens, it's probably not your **responsibility**
to make them **better.** Let the grown-ups be in charge
of this. They will take your pet to the vet or give them some
sort of **treatment.**

Your job is to make your pet **feel better** and let them
know that you love them. There are lots of different ways you can
do this but the main methods are:

Cuddling
Drawing Pictures Of Them
Telling Them Stories

The best stories you can tell them are ones you make up about
them. If you can't think of anything, however, I have written a
story you can use. It's about **mice** but has a **happy
ending** so most pets should like it.

Trouble
with pets:
Page 54

The vets:
Page 225

James' sick
pet story:
Page 120

Dogs

Ooh. I love dogs! When I see a dog I go all **gooey** inside and I can't help but stare at it. If I visit someone's house and it turns out they have a dog, I spend the whole time trying to attract the dog's attention and get it to like me. Dogs are like **furry children** that don't talk. I love them!

Dogs come in all sorts of shapes and sizes. There are small dogs like **Chihuahuas** and giant dogs like **Great Danes.** If you search for 'dog breeds' you'll find all sorts of **strange** dog breeds.

Apparently, in terms of weight, you could fit 87 Chihuahuas inside a Great Dane. Also, Chihuahuas playing with Great Danes are the funniest thing on Earth. Look up 'Fearless Chihuahua plays with Puzzled Great Dane' online.

There are many other **types of dogs** in between. In various parts of this book you'll find pages on many dogs including Labradors, sausage dogs, Airedale Terriers and spaniels.

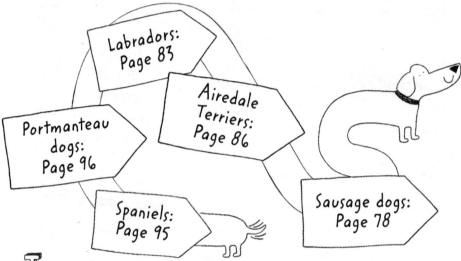

Labradors:
Page 83

Airedale
Terriers:
Page 86

Portmanteau
dogs:
Page 96

Spaniels:
Page 95

Sausage dogs:
Page 78

There are also some new types of dogs which are made up of half one breed of dog and half another breed of dog. I like to call these **portmanteau dogs.**

Dogs are a great example of a domesticated animal – which means that they are very good at doing the laundry and loading the dishwasher. My dog is very **helpful** around the house and pre-cleans all of our dinner plates by covering them in **dog saliva.**

Believe it or not, dogs are all descended from **wolves.** There are **hundreds** of different dog breeds and every single one of them used to be a particular kind of wolf. If you want to find out more about this:

All dogs are descended from wolves: Page 106

Beginning page: Page 9

Feeding a pet: Page 22

Some people like **big dogs.** Some people like **little dogs.** If you want to find out what I think about it:

Small dogs V big dogs: Page 94

Dogs and fires

Something you might notice about dogs is how close they can sit to a **fire**.

If you try to put your hand where the dog's nose is, your hand will **burn**. So how does a dog manage to sit so close to the fire without **melting** or **bursting into flames** or getting hotter and **hotter** and **HOTTER** until eventually it just goes:

Woof

I did some research about this and found a woman called **Marjory**, who said she had six Labradors and three fireplaces in her house. Marjory agreed that her Labradors can sit very close to a fire without **over-heating**. She says that dogs must have heat-proof noses or there is some sort of **sprinkler system** which keeps the nose wet and stops it from catching fire.

'Every good dog-owner knows that a dog's nose should always be **wet,**' she said. 'If it's not wet, the dog might be **unwell** and also, it might burst into flames. That's what I think, anyway.'

If dogs really do have **heat-proof** noses they would be a bit like **space shuttles** and you could fire a dog through space. Why would you want to fire a dog through space? Maybe if you were on the **Moon** and you needed to send a message back to Earth. Maybe if you were on holiday – **on the Moon.**

And then you got **stuck** there because you missed the last bus home. You'd be worried you would run out of **oxygen.** You would need to send a message back home.

Then you notice that there is a space **catapult** for firing things back to earth. You wonder what's the **best** thing to fire through space. You **volunteer** but your Dad says you would burn up when you hit the Earth's atmosphere.

Holidays on the Moon: Page 148

Things you can fire with a space catapult: Page 164

Then you notice your two **spaniels**. 'Of course! Dogs have heat-proof noses. They would be fine.'

Your first spaniel volunteers by **wagging** her tail so you fit her into the space catapult. Dad works the controls by pressing **buttons,** adjusting the position of the levers and scratching the inside of his nose.

We all get more and more **excited** and eventually a huge sign flickers into life, glowing with the words

READY TO FIRE...

We all dance around in **excitement**.

Dad presses the button on the **Bucheto Lunar Space Catapult 2000** and suddenly it makes a noise like a buffalo doing a **bottom burp** in a wheelie bin. And then with a whoosh and a howl, our Spaniel is **catapulted** into space towards Earth. Dad pulls out some handy cosmic binoculars and watches your dog's progress through space.

Pet toilet behaviour: Page 28

Me: Is she all right? What's she doing?

Dad: She's flying through space incredibly quickly. And now she's circling the Moon.

Me: Why is she doing that?

Dad: She's just looking for somewhere to do a wee.

Me: What's she doing now?

Dad: She is heading towards the Earth's atmosphere.

Me: Oh no. Will she be okay? Or will she get too hot and burst into flames?

Dad: I don't know. No, wait! She's hit the Earth's atmosphere!

Me: Is she okay?

Dad: Her nose is glowing red! There are flames coming out of the side of her nose!

Me: Is she okay?

Dad: Oh she's fine actually. She's fine because

SHE HAS A HEATPROOF NOSE!

The space people pick her up on their radar and say:

'Is it a bird? Is it a plane? No. It's a spaniel.

Welcome, dog from the Moon.

What message do you bring?'

And then the dog would say...

The trouble is you can't teach a dog to say, 'My family are stuck on the Moon. Please help them.' And you can't write the message on a piece of paper and stick it in her collar, can you? It would **burn** up.

Hopefully you would have a **spare dog** – another spaniel. You would load her into the Bucheto Lunar Space Catapult 2000 but this time you would shave a **message** in her fur.

Or you could just shave an 'S' on one **buttock** and another 'S' on the other. Then, when the people at the space station lift up her tail it would clearly say **SOS**.

What you can teach your pets to do: Page 37

All dogs are descended from wolves: Page 106

Sausage dogs

Sausage dogs or **wieners** are the nicknames for **Dachshunds**. They are famous for having long, sausage-shaped bodies and tiny little legs.

What I want to know though, is this: do sausage dogs eat **sausages?** Or do they just look at them and say, 'I'm not eating that. It looks like my **Granny!'**

In certain parts of the world, people like to indulge in the exciting **sport** of Bopping Dogs On The Head With Sausages. This is a lot more fun than it sounds, **trust me.**

Bopping dogs on the head wth sausages: Page 100

Dogs that are named after food: Page 206

Someone in your house is allergic to your pet: Page 235

Tummy tickling

Dogs love having their tummies **tickled.** Some dogs don't even wait until they reach you before they lie on their back. They **roll** right over before they get anywhere near you and fly the last part of their journey **upside down.**

Dogs want you to tickle them for **hours** and **hours.** They would happily be tickled all day if you had the energy. The world record for a dog having its tummy tickled is held by Roxy — a standard **poodle** — who was tickled by a team of twelve **firemen** from North Wales for six and a half days before eventually throwing in the towel and having a **biscuit.**

Record-breaking
pets:
Page 211

One of the biggest **differences** between cats and dogs is tummy tickling. Dogs **adore** having their tummies tickled but with **cats,** it's a little more complicated. Cats will let you tickle them but then events can quickly get out of hand...

First of all, they **lie** in front of you.

So you tickle them and what do they do? They **attack** you. That's what they do! This is what happens if you try and tickle a cat's **tummy.**

Tickle my tummy — if you dare

I thought it wanted me to tickle its tummy but then it beat me up.

Claws, teeth, fangs, weapons. All of these things work together to get as much **blood** out of a person as possible. You will then find that it is almost completely **impossible** to remove the cat from your arm once it has attached itself to you.

How do you get the thing off? You **can't.**

Here are some of the ways I have tried to **remove** a cat from my arm.

1. Running cold water on it.

2. Growing a potato on its head.

3. Taping it to a space rocket.

81

There is literally **no way** to remove a cat from your arm once you have tried to tickle it. The only thing you can do is **wait** until you are incredibly old and the cat has **died.**

Search on YouTube for 'How To Tickle A Cat' and you'll see for yourself how **ferocious** these furry animals can get!

Dogs:
Page 69

Game-pet
chart:
Page 48

Being attacked by
cats: why have you
got scratches on your
face?: Page 156

Cats V Dogs:
Page 221

Labradors

One of my **favourite** types of dogs is the **Labrador** or **retriever.**

They come in different **colours.**

Golden Retriever

Black Labrador

When they are puppies, Labradors are possibly the **cutest** things in the world. Apart from possibly Princess Kate, the Duchess of Cambridge. Actually, Princess Kate and Labrador puppies are quite similar. They both have big eyes, glossy hair and lots of **teeth.**

Chocolate Labrador

Notice also how their freckles are in exactly the same places.

When Labradors get old though, nobody wants them any more. Labrador puppies are adorable. Labrador elderlies are **fat** and **smelly.** No one wants to cuddle them and they just lie in front of the cooker all day, looking sad and releasing deadly rotten **bottom bombs.**

The **best** thing about a Labrador is its **tail.** Most dogs, when they are **happy,** wag their tail. Little dogs tend to stand or sit still and their tail goes from side to side.

Made-up types of dog: Page 150

Here is a small dog being happy.

The Labrador, however, is different. When
a Labrador is happy its
head stays still and
then the rest of the
body wags!

Here is a
Labrador
being happy.

The best thing about the
Labrador's tail is how joyfully
destructive it is. They **damage** so much but with
such happiness. Without even knowing what they are doing.
At the front they are **smiling** but at the back they are
knocking over cups of coffee, smashing precious ornaments and
whacking small children in the face! Search for the video
called 'Little Dog Gets Whacked by a Wagging Tail'
on YouTube and experience
this damage and destruction
for yourself!

Labrador:
Page 83

Things that pets
have destroyed:
Page 220

Airedale Terriers

You may have heard it said that the human body is 70% water. Well, the Airedale Terrier is 99% air.

Originally bred in Yorkshire for hunting **clouds,** the Airedale is the only inflatable dog in the **world.**

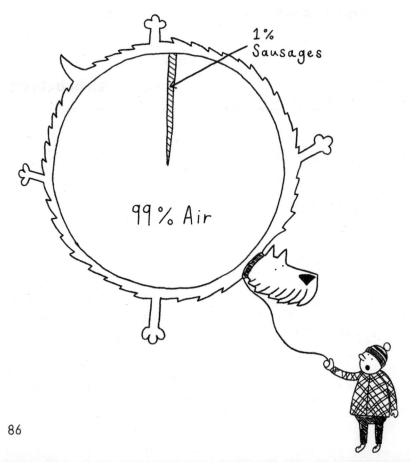

1%
Sausages

99% Air

Airedale Terriers are extremely **rare.** This is mainly because they have a habit of slipping out of their collars and floating off into **space** – never to be seen again. But there are rumours that a group of Airedales have formed a **colony** on the Moon and are living there quite happily, earning a living by running a **crazy golf** centre.

Holidays on the Moon: Page 148

The Airedale Air Museum: Page 168

If you're ever in Yorkshire, the Airedale Air Museum contains a wonderful **exhibition** about the Airedale Terrier and how it was used not only for hunting clouds but also as a substitute for **kites,** during the 1940s kite shortage.

There are some other **inflatable** pets.

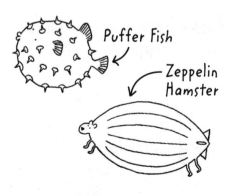

Puffer Fish

Zeppelin Hamster

Pump-up Kitten

Chihuahuas

The Chihuahua is officially the world's most **difficult** dog in the world to spell. In a survey of eleven-year-olds from a primary school in Salford, only **5%** could spell it correctly. Here are some of the other attempts.

Chi wow wah: 6%

tchoo woo woo: 2%

Chuwhuaha: 3%

Chichiwahwah: 13%

Shaw ah wahoo was: 5%

Cherhuawa: 7%

Chewauahahahauahauahauah: 18%

I don't want to be a part of this ridiculous test: 25%

A group of 100 university **professors** were also asked. Even though they were some of the **cleverest** people in the world, only 9% of them knew how to spell Chihuahua correctly.

Strangely enough, more than 11% of those clever professors thought it was just an **imaginary** dog and therefore couldn't be spelled at all.

The Chihuahua is, of course, from **Mexico** and so yesterday I phoned a man in Mexico to ask him how to spell Chihuahua. He said that he didn't know how to spell Chihuahua either and he lived in a place that was called **Chihuahua** so you would think he would know.

As a final **survey** I asked 100 actual Chihuahuas how to spell Chihuahua.

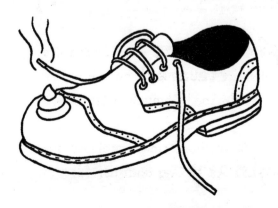

23% of them said woof

32% of them were asleep

47% of them did a teeny tiny poo on my shoe

Pet toilet behaviour: Page 28

All dogs are descended from wolves: Page 106

The wild ponies of Caenlochan

A couple of years ago I was **camping** in the Scottish mountains and decided to walk to the Caenlochan Glen with my dog. Mrs Miggins is the best **mountain climbing** dog. Ever. So far she has climbed over 40 Scottish mountains.

After a while it got so dark I couldn't see where to go next. So I pitched my tent, made some dinner and went to sleep.

But in the middle of the night I was woken by **snuffling** and **snorting** noises. I poked my head out of the door to see a group of wild horses had surrounded my tent. I got out and told them to go away but the big **stallion** horse would not leave. He was very **angry** about me sleeping in his field, I think.

Snuffle
Snuffle

Snort
Snort

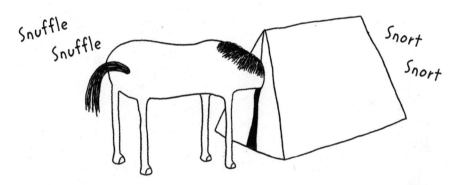

Now, these weren't nice ponies that someone **owns** and looks after. These were wild ponies that belong to no one and I was scared. The stallion stood there scraping at the ground with his foot, snorting and worst of all — doing massive **bottom-burps.**

I was a two hour walk from my car, there was no **phone reception** and I was on my own (apart from Mrs Miggins). Eventually, I got out a saucepan and a spoon and made as much noise as I could, by **banging** the spoon on the saucepan.

BANG!

FAAART

After about half an hour of me banging, and him farting and snorting, he got **bored** and went away.

I didn't **sleep** very well that night.

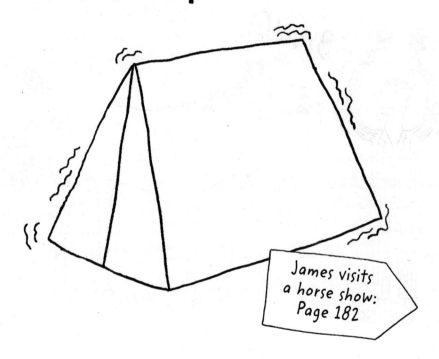

James visits a horse show: Page 182

Small dogs versus big dogs

As a rule I like big dogs more than little dogs. Big dogs are usually quite **cool**. Small dogs are **yappy** and annoying. Big dogs like lying down and having their tummies tickled.

Little dogs like **chasing** cars. But why do little dogs chase cars? It's not like they're going to catch one. We should make **motorbikes** for little dogs. Then they could chase cars and yap and actually catch a car.

I don't know what a small dog would do if it **actually** caught a car. Probably just **yap** at it.

Tummy tickling: Page 79

Pets that go bonkers: Page 58

Spaniels

Spaniels are **awesome.** Usually, their ears are bigger than their head. This makes them look very **cute** but not very **intelligent.**

It is difficult to take someone **seriously** if their ears are bigger than their head. Imagine if your teacher had ears like that. Would you **listen** to anything she ever said?

Some spaniels have such **big ears** that if they turn their heads really quickly they actually hit themselves in the face with their own ears. Other

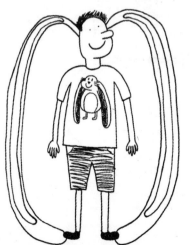

spaniels have ears that are so long that when they walk around **sniffing** for stuff they accidentally stand on their own ears. Imagine if **you** could **stand** on your own ears.

Famous pets throughout history: Page 132

Portmanteau dogs

It's always nice to meet dogs that are half one type of dog and half another type. They used to be called **'cross'**. For example, 'My dog is a border collie cross Labrador'.

It always makes me **laugh** when someone says that they have a cross German Shepherd because I just imagine a really angry German man standing in a field **shouting** at sheep.

But now, cross breed dogs have become **fashionable** and **expensive** and are called things like...

Famous pets throughout history: Page 132

Illegal things you still can't do on a horse: Page 110

Sprockets

Cocker-Poos

Labra-wow-wows

Don't tell anyone but some of those dogs were actually made-up.

Yorkshire Wolfhounds

Border-Weillers

I like to call these sorts of dogs **portmanteau dogs,** after portmanteau words, which were invented by **Lewis Carroll.**

My favourite **portmanteau** dog is the Labradoodle. The Labradoodle is half Labrador and half poodle, which apparently makes it **hypo-allergenic** and **really expensive.**

Pet allergies: Page 192

Now, according to some **research** that I pretended to do, when you cross two animals there are usually two ways of naming their children. If you cross lions and tigers, for example, you either get a **Tigon** or a **Liger.** It depends which animal is the mum and which is the dad.

If the dad is a lion and the mum is a tiger you get a **Tigon.** Like this:

If the dad is a tiger and the mum is a lion you get a **Liger.** Like this:

So a **Labradoodle** must have a dad who is a poodle and a mum who is a labrador.

If it was the **other** way around you would get...

A POOHADOR!

To me that sounds much more **exciting.** It sounds less like a dog and more like a **weird** kind of Spanish sport. The sort of sport where you stand in the middle of a circle of sand and people throw **poo** at you.

Oh no actually, that's not a Spanish sport. That's **nursery school.**

Weird sports:
Page 218

Things that pets
have destroyed:
Page 220

Bopping dogs on the head with sausages

I am a big fan of **unusual** sports. Every year I go to the Felixstowe Fish Throwing Festival.

If I can, I always make an effort to take my family **piglet bowling** on a Sunday afternoon.

My favourite unusual sport, however, is...

Bopping Dogs On The Head With Sausages

If you have a dog, a lot of sausages that you don't need and literally nothing better to do, you might want to try this unusual sport.

I invented this sport in **Australia** when I was very bored. I was hosting an extremely long and **dull show** where I had to spend the whole day introducing old ladies singing songs about **fish,** mums dancing in badly-fitting **leotards** and angry men reading poems about **shoes.**

In between all this, I tried to keep the audience **awake.** I got on to the subject about how **difficult** it is to bop a dog on the head with a sausage.

This is because before the sausage has had time to make **contact** with the dog's head, the dog will open its mouth and eat it.

There were lots of dogs at this **festival** and a hot dog stand! I persuaded the hot dog stand to give us some sausages and got a local **radio station** to announce the world's first 'Bopping Your Dog On The Head With A Sausage Competition.'

It was a great **success** and was won by a man and his **blind terrier.**

If you want to start your own **competition** simply get lots of friends to come over with their dogs and fry up some sausages. Wait until the sausages go cold and then see who is the first to get three sausages to meet their dog's **forehead.**

102

If you wanted you could even make a **campfire** and cook the sausages on that. **Yummy.**

How to make a campfire: Page 140

Sausage dogs: Page 78

Weird sports: Page 218

Bopping dogs on the head with sausages is very **popular** in Mexico, where they use **Chihuahuas** and **Chipolatas.**

Game-pet cart: Page 48

Dogs rubbing their bums along the ground

Every now and again you will notice your dog sitting down with its back legs pointing **upwards,** using its front feet to shuffle along the carpet. When it does this it usually has a very **strange expression** on its face. If dogs could speak, I think it would be saying:

I know this is weird but I just can't help myself.

Rubbing their **bums** along the ground is one of the **funniest** things dogs can do. If you have never seen one do it, please search for *'Funny Compilation of Dogs Wiping Their Bums'*. It is bonkers!

But **why** are they doing it? It's **probably** one of the following things:

1. **T**hey are wiping their **bum** on your mum's carpet.

2. **T**hey have an **itchy** bum and are trying to scratch it. (On your mum's carpet.)

3. **T**hey are really **bored** and so they are playing a game that only dogs can understand. (Using your mum's carpet.)

4. **T**hey are trying to **entertain** you by doing an **impression** of a Christmas turkey. (Whilst ruining your mum's carpet.)

Trouble with pets:
Page 54

All dogs are descended from wolves

That's right. It's hard to believe when you look at a **Chihuahua,** but all dogs are great-great-great... a lot of greats... grandchildren of **wolves.**

Apparently, some **wolves** started following people around about 130,000 years ago, wanting to be pets. Over time, we started to **breed** the wolves, choosing different ones to have puppies to make all the different sorts of dog we wanted. Some people wanted little dogs, others big ones. Some wanted **friendly** dogs to look after their children. Others wanted scary dogs to keep their **enemies** away.

Chihuahuas: Page 88

How to make a campfire: Page 140

Dogs and fires: Page 72

Different types of dogs came from different personalities of wolves. In a **wild** wolf pack each wolf has a particular job to do. Some wolves have an **amazing** sense of smell and it's their job to sniff out prey like rabbits and deer. The grandchildren of these wolves are now the **sniffer** dogs: bloodhounds and spaniels etc.

Some wolves had the job of rounding up the **prey** and keeping it together. These wolves became collies and sheep dogs. And other wolves had the job of **chasing** the prey. They were super **fast** and their descendants are greyhounds and whippets.

I'm not sure what kind of wolf **descended** into the big-eared furry fool who rubs its bum along my carpet and then sits in a corner and eats my **pyjamas...**

But maybe even a wolf pack needs a **wolf** to make all the others laugh. That's the sort of wolf I would be, I suppose.

Things that pets have destroyed: page 220

Dogs: Page 69

Great Danes

The **largest** real dog in the world is the Great Dane. The largest made-up dog in the world is the **Triple Burger Dog.** This breed is found in fast food restaurants and is descended from relatively small, **scavenger** dogs which ate leftovers from the skips behind hot dog stands. Over hundreds of years, they grew **larger** and **larger** on a high protein and fat diet. These days most Triple Burger Dogs have been rounded up and put in special kennels the size of houses. But some of these **magnificent** beasts can still be found **lurking** in the car parks of fast food restaurants waiting to **pounce** not just on a customer's food but on the customer.

Portmanteau dogs: Page 96

The Great Dane is truly **massive** and was originally bred for working in piano factories but is now mainly used by house movers for shifting **refrigerators** and other large pieces of **furniture.**

The Great Dane is often confused with one of Shakespeare's plays called **Hamlet.** Hamlet is the name of the Prince of Denmark and people from Denmark are called **Danes.** So Hamlet is often called 'the Great Dane' by people in the theatre.

So if you want a Great Dane, make sure you don't get one from a **theatre person.** You might accidentally get a bloke in tights talking about how he can't decide whether to be a **bee** or not.

Who is Shakespeare and why should I give a cat's bum about him?: Page 142

Dogs: Page 69

Pets that can do jobs: Page 172

Illegal things you still can't do on a horse

Most people use horses for having **fun** in some way but many horses throughout history have been used for **criminal purposes...**

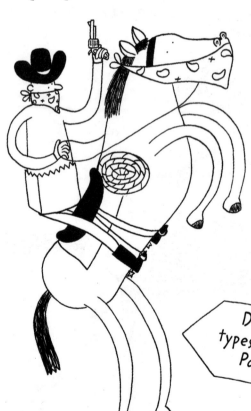

In the Wild West many **cowboys** used to steal horses. This was known as **rustling** and had nothing to do with wearing brown paper bags instead of underpants. **Dick Turpin** was a famous highway robber that used a horse to rob people.

Different types of horse: Page 20

The wild ponies of Caenlochan: Page 90

Lady Godiva famously rode around **naked** on a horse. According to research Lady Godiva lived in the **13th century** and to protest against taxation, she rode naked through the streets of Coventry on her horse, only covered by her long hair. Everyone was **very shocked** by this at the time. (These days she would probably get a **round of applause** and a **biscuit.**)

The people of **Airedale** claim their own version of **Lady Godiva.** According to the Airedale Air Museum a lady called Susan Spot-Weld rode naked through the streets of Bingley in **1974** as a protest against something or other but apparently it was on a **bicycle** so maybe that shouldn't be in this book.

The Airedale Air Museum: Page 168

Things that shouldn't be in this book: Page 239

Portmanteau dogs: Page 96

Ponies: Page 178

According to the **laws** of England doing anything **illegal** on a horse is **still illegal.** There is nothing that is against the law that is okay to do if you do it on a horse, apart from entering a **horse race.** (Entering a horse race without a horse is illegal!)

The following things, however, are **particularly illegal** if done on a horse and in some countries can get you sent to **prison** for life.

1. Going up a footpath – whilst on a horse.
2. Travelling faster than 70mph – whilst on a horse.
3. Fishing for cod without a license – whilst on a horse.
4. Vandalising a bus stop – whilst on a horse and dressed as Sir Lancelot.
5. Making lists of things that aren't true – whilst on a horse.

Things that come from South America

Guinea pigs famously come from **South America.** But what else comes from there?

Well, a lot of raw materials like **aluminium** and **copper** come from South America. There's a dance called the **Tango.** That comes from South America too. South America also has the **Amazon rainforest** right in the middle of it. So a lot of our **oxygen** comes from South America. We should probably help them look after it as best we can.

One of the most exciting pets that come from South America is the **Chinchilla.** This is a small and extremely fluffy animal that looks a bit like a **hat with legs.** Chinchillas are extremely **cute** but they aren't in this book very much. If you want to see some **chinchillas in action,** search for 'Chinchilla Compilation — Fluffy, Cute and Funny Chinchillas — PlushCompilations'. They are **ridiculously cute.**

Pets which aren't in this book much: Page 236

Impossible Imaginary Pets: Page 227

115

Made-up types of fish

There are literally **thousands** of different types of fish. Some of them sound so **ridiculous** that they must be **made-up.** Some of them really are made-up. Here are some fish I have invented.

THE BLUE EYED STROPPY

This is a really **moody** fish that looks at people in a funny way with its bright blue eyes.

THE LOLLIPOP LADY FISH

This is a **luminous,** yellowy-green creature which stops other fish from bumping into each other.

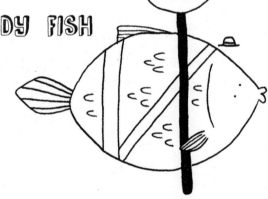

SPOONFISH

This fish is used by other fish as a **sneaky way** of eating **yoghurt.**

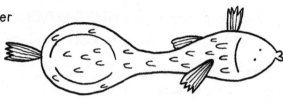

HALLOUMI CHEESE FISH

Squeaks if you eat it.

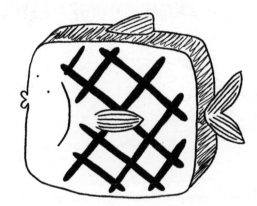

Royal Society for Made-Up Animals: Page 174

Goldfish: Page 196

Holidays on the Moon: Page 148

Cats

Cats are strange, furry little creatures that almost certainly come from **another planet.**

Something you must definitely **NOT** do with cats is **juggle** with them. It's almost **impossible** and they will get very angry. It is much more manageable to start with **kittens** and then work your way up to full-sized cats.

IF YOU JUGGLE ME, I WILL DESTROY YOU.

HOW TO BE MORE EMPATHETIC

What on Earth is Latin and why should I give a hamster's poo about it?: Page 212

Cats have many **unusual** features and habits. One of these is that their tongue is made out of **sandpaper** and if you can persuade one to lick your feet you will giggle and giggle and giggle until you **actually melt.** Cats love **licking feet** so much they will do it for ten minutes straight!

This is **not a lie!** Look up 'Cat Licks Toes for Ten Minutes' online.

Different types of cat: Page 124

Litter trays: Page 28

Beginning Page: Page 9

Ten things you didn't know about cats: Page 131

James' sick pet story

It can be very **difficult** if your pet is **poorly**. Something you can do for it is read it a **story**.

Try this story that I have written **especially** for the occasion.

Once upon a time there was a family of **mice** who lived in a field. The mice were very **happy** and loved curling up in their nest and having **farting** competitions.

One day, however, a **terrible noise** startled the mice. Other mice started running past them and they realised that the field was being **harvested.** Quickly they packed up their belongings and started running.

Soon they were out of the field and stumbled upon an old **barn.** There were plenty of **gaps** in the walls so the mice had no difficulty getting in. Once inside they made a home from the straw, and bits and bobs lying around inside the barn.

One day the door to the barn opened and in came an **old man.** The mice all scuttled away and found hiding places. They watched as the old man went over to a huge **brown sheet** that was draped over something quite large in the corner of the barn.

It turned out to be an old **classic car** that the old man was rebuilding. Every morning for months and months, the old man would come to the barn and work on his car. He would **unbolt** one bit and replace it with another bit. He would **polish** things, **twiddle** with things, **solder** and **weld.**

As time went by the mice became more **curious,** getting closer and closer to the old man and his work. One day, the inevitable happened. The **old man** saw one of the mice.

'Good Lord,' he said. 'What do we have here? It's a little mouse sharing the barn with my car.' The mouse was very **scared** but the old man was kind. 'I think I will have to make you a little home, won't I?'

The old man made a **box** from wood and filled it with **straw** so that the mouse family could have a proper house. He placed the box so they could watch him tinker with his car through the **windows** of their new home.

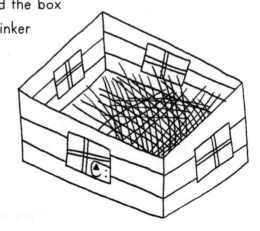

The mice became fascinated with the **tools** and **nuts and bolts** he was using and eventually they were able to help him by getting the correct sized spanner or ratchet. After six months, the car was **complete,** thanks to the old man's hard work and the mice's help.

'I couldn't have done this without you,' said the old man to the mice as they gazed at the **shiny red car** in front of them. 'We should all go for a drive.'

And so, the mice all climbed in and the old man drove them to the **seaside** where they had ice cream and hot dogs.

Maybe they went on other **adventures** as well — maybe you could make up these adventures and tell them to your **poorly pet.**

My pet is sick: Page 68

The vets: Page 225

Different types of cat

Some people call them **moggies,** some people (not many) call them **furry whisker turtles.** You can find out all about the different breeds on the Internet or in the library.

My favourites are...

Burmese, Balinese, Himalayans and **Norwegian Forest Cats.**

What on Earth are libraries?: Page 159

Burmese

Balinese

Himalayan

Norwegian Forest Cat

The **Norwegian Forest Cat** should not be confused with the completely made-up Norwegian Wood Cat. I once had a **Norwegian Wood Cat.** Or should I say, it once had me? The thing completely took over my life and I had to sleep in the bath.

Made-up types of cat: Page 216

Getting a kitten

Getting a **kitten** is very **exciting.** The main thing to do is to help the thing settle in so you need to give it lots of **love and cuddles.**

Some people put **butter** on their kitten's **paws.** It doesn't matter what's going on in a cat's life, licking butter off its own paws will make it **happy.** Look up 'cat licks butter' online and you'll see it yourself. You could experiment with other spreads... I wonder if a kitten would like having **cream cheese** on its feet. I know I do.

Don't welcome your new kitten to your home by offering it a **cucumber.** Apparently cats are terrified of them.

Safe and ethical experiments you can do with your pets: Page 40

Are cats afraid of cucumbers?: Page 66

More unusual features and habits of cats

Cats might be small and fluffy but they think they are **ninjas.** Your cat might be called Flopsy or Mister Bumcushion but in their own minds they are actually called **Dark Angel** or **Night Stalker.**

Ten things you didn't know about cats: Page 131

One of the most **unusual** things about cats is their **eyelids.** If you look at a cat closely you will notice that they don't blink. Ever. Try having a **staring contest** with a cat. You can't win. After about 20 seconds you will have **tears** streaming down your face and the cat will just be sitting there looking **smug.**

This is because cats have **see-through eyelids,** which is like a third eyelid known as a 'nicitating **membrane'.** That's right. They are blinking all the time but we can't see it! Search for a video called 'epic cat stare'.

Another **weird** thing about cats is that their tongue feels like **sandpaper.** Try letting a cat lick your hand. It's like being attacked by a **Christmas tree.**

The reason cats have a tongue like this is so they can use it as a kind of **velcro** for sticking their faces to brick walls.

Probably the most **famous** thing that everyone knows about cats is that they always land on their **feet.** This is because their **backs** have a clever way of **twisting round** so that they always put their **feet down.**

Having said that, if you go on the Internet and search for 'epic cat fails' (as far as I can tell the Internet was invented so that people could watch videos of cats being **stupid**), you will find lots of evidence showing cats not landing on their feet.

At all.

And finally, cats do a weird thing with their **paws** when they are sitting on you. They kind of **massage** you, one paw after the other. Apparently, this is because they think they will get **milk** out of you like this. This shows you just how **weird** cats really are.

Feeding a pet: Page 22

Playing with pets: Page 36

Pets that go bonkers: Page 58

Brilliant names for all sorts of pets

Can't decide what to call your pet? Here is my **guide** to **pet naming:**

The most popular names for dogs are **Bailey** and **Max.** But you can do better than that. What about Deefer, as in **Deefer Dog?** Or why not name your pet after your favourite movie or book character? Why not have a hamster called **Voldemort** or a guinea pig called **Chewbacca?**

Everyone will tease me.

In my opinion, all cats should be called either **Mr Fluffywhuffkins** or **Santa Claws.** If I had a pet sheep or goat I would call it **Cardinal Wolsey.**

Playing Connect 4 with your pet: Page 48

Ten things you didn't know about cats: Page 131

Hamster conspiracy theory: Page 222

Ten things you didn't know about cats

1. Cats are afraid of **cucumbers.**

2. Cats are all descended from **aliens.**

3. Cats aren't actually cats. They are more closely related to **beetles** than anything else.

> Are cats afraid of cucumbers?: Page 66

4. 46% of all cats are called Mr Fluffy Whuffkins. The other 54% are called **Simon.**

5. The best name for a cat is **Ceefer.**

> Brilliant names for all sorts of pets: Page 130

6. Most cats would discover they actually like **dogs** if they would only take the time to get to know them.

7. Cats are allergic to **doughnuts.**

8. Some cats can meow the **alphabet backwards.**

9. If you run out of **kitchen roll,** a cat can be used to mop up spilt liquids and food.

10. Cats can be trained to **dance** to music, just like horses.

Famous pets throughout history

Admiral **Lord Nelson** had a pet guinea pig called **Trafalgar,** which he used to keep inside his jacket. In most of the pictures you find of Nelson you can see him reaching between his buttons to give his guinea pig a cheeky **tickle.**

Lord Byron was a **poet,** long distance swimmer and collector of **weird pets.** Apparently he once had a **pet giraffe** in his house and when he went to Cambridge University (which is basically a big school) he took his **pet bear** with him.

HIS PET BEAR!

Try looking this up on the **Internet** or in a **library**. How do you keep a bear at school? Did it have its **own room** or did he keep it in his **locker?**

I once tried to take some **tadpoles** to school and half of them fell out of the bowl on the walk to school. The other half looked **sad** on the **windowsill** for a couple of weeks and I wondered if I should flush them down the loo or release them into the **school pond.**

And that was just **tadpoles.** How on Earth would you look after a **bear** at school?

Maybe Byron kept the bear in his **bathtub?**

Complications caused by keeping animals in the bath: Page 56

Or maybe he trained him to give him a **big hug** and stay really still so he could pretend it was his **winter coat.**

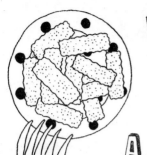

What would your pet bear eat? Would it eat all of the **fish fingers** at lunchtime?

Another famous pet owner was the **Maharaja of Junagadh** – rather wonderfully, he had **800 dogs** and no slippers.

King **Charles II** loved his **dog** so much that he began to look like it. (This does happen to a lot of people.)

Feeding a pet: Page 22

Portmanteau dogs: Page 96

People who copied their look from their dog: Page 176

Tiger sharks

BARBARA FROM DEVON KEEPS TIGER SHARKS IN HER BATH

'I was going to get some goldfish,' says Barbara. 'But I found these beauties on a specialist website. They were so cute I just had to buy some.'

That's how Barbara ended up impractically keeping tiger sharks in her bath. Barbara lives in Seaton, Devon with her elderly mother, three cats and two fully-grown tiger sharks.

In the wild, tiger sharks eat a wide range of foods including crustaceans, fish, seals, birds, squid, turtles and even dolphins.

Barbara, however, feeds her tiger sharks cat food, cheesecake and those smelly, frothy bath bomb things you buy your mum for Mother's Day.

Tiger sharks do have excellent eyesight, so one of the downsides of keeping tiger sharks in the bathtub is that when Barbara is having a shower she always feels like she is being watched.

'On the plus side, however,' says Barbara, 'I do love looking at them when I'm sitting on the loo. It's very relaxing to see them circle around menacingly in the tub and when one of them leaps into the air with its teeth out, it really get things moving in the bottom department if you know what I mean.'

Barbara is so pleased with her tiger sharks that she is thinking of getting herself a pair of great white sharks to join them. I asked her if she thought there was enough room for any more sharks.

'Hmm,' she said, biting her bottom lip. 'I think we're going to need a bigger bath!'

Complications caused by keeping animals in the bath: Page 56

Hamsters

The Latin name for hamster is **Cricetinae.**

What on Earth is Latin and why should I give a hamster's poo about it?: Page 212

More about nits: Page 214

Which-Pet-Flow-Chart: Page 18

Hamsters are probably the **cheapest** pets you can buy (with the possible exception of **nits**). Hamsters also take up the least amount of space (with the possible exception of nits).

nits

Hamsters are the **perfect** pet for people who don't have much space. Maybe you live in a town or maybe you don't have a garden. But really — hamsters are suitable for almost everyone. Check the **Which-Pet-Flow-Chart** to see if a hamster is the right pet for you.

The main **problem** with hamsters is that they don't live very long. They also have a tendency to **breed** really quickly...

They can, however, be trained to run through your hair and **eat** all your nits.

Made-up types of hamster

There are only **three** types of hamster in the whole world:

1. Hyperactive

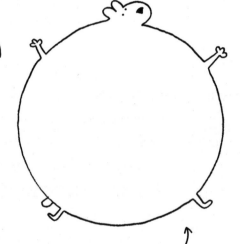

2. Explosive

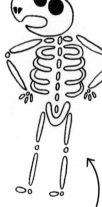

3. Dead

Royal Society for Made-Up Animals: Page 174

Your pet dies: Page 233

How to make a campfire

The most important thing about making a campfire is **being safe.** You must **not** do any of this without the help of a responsible grown-up. Human beings have been making fires for tens of thousands of years. Recently though, lots of people seem to have **forgotten** how to do it. The best way to learn is to ask an expert to teach you. The basics however are as follows...

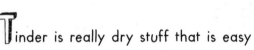
How to test if a grown-up is responsible: Page 198

Make sure you have **permission** from the people who own the land you're on. Next, gather everything you need for the first half hour of fire burning. You will need **tinder, kindling, sticks** and **fat sticks.**

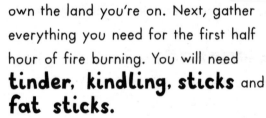

Tinder is really dry stuff that is easy to light. Paper is good, or handfuls of really dry grass, or bark from trees. **Kindling** is a handful of tiny twigs.

Make a **safe space** for the fire to be in. A circle of stones is good. Then, make a pile of tinder and light it with a match and the help of a **responsible** grown-up. Add bits of kindling slowly, being **careful** not to burn yourself.

Carefully add larger and larger sticks until you have a decent sized fire. And remember, the **wise person** builds a small fire and keeps warm. The unwise person builds a large fire and keeps warm fetching wood for it. Or, as this is a book about **pets** maybe that should be:

The cat builds a small fire and keeps warm. The dog builds a large fire and keeps warm fetching sticks.

Be warned: as soon as you light a fire, a dog will appear from nowhere and get in front of it. They just **can't help it.**

Dogs and fires: Page 72

Who is Shakespeare and why should I give a cat's bum about him?

You hear an awful lot about **Shakespeare.**

> Shakespeare wrote plays and poems in the late 16th century and the early 17th century.

Plays like *Macbeth* and *Romeo and Juliet* are very popular and if you haven't come across his work yet, trust me, you will. **Millions** of books have been written about Shakespeare so I won't try and tell you too much. If you want to know more just look him up on the Internet or ask in a **library.**

What on Earth are libraries?: Page 159

I will just tell you five things about Shakespeare that I know:

1. He didn't shake pears at anyone ever. But he did once **wobble an orange.**

2. My favourite play of his is called *King Lear* and my favourite character is the **Fool.** In fact the Fool was partly the inspiration for what I do for a job.

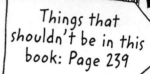

Things that shouldn't be in this book: Page 239

Great Danes: Page 108

3. Lots of Shakespeare's plays are written in **verse** with a particular kind of **rhythm** to it, which is very interesting.

4. There is nothing **posh** about Shakespeare. Don't let posh people put you off Shakespeare. In fact, don't let **posh people** put you off anything.

5. In his plays, Shakespeare has somehow managed to cover all the different parts of what it is to be **human.** Jealousy, loneliness, love, fear, ambition — everything really. If you are ever suffering from any human **emotion,** ask someone who knows about Shakespeare, to point you towards the bit of Shakespeare that will help you understand what you are **feeling.**

Life expectancy of hamsters

Now, although hamsters make **wonderful** pets, they do have one small **drawback.** Hamsters do not live for very long. On average they last for about **two years** but to be honest, you're lucky if you can get one home from the shop without it dying.

When I was your age, I had a pet hamster and my hamster lasted for just **half an hour.** As research for this book I have asked many people how long their hamsters lasted and some of them claim to have had hamsters that lasted **five years** and sometimes even **six** years.

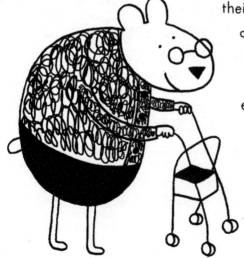

OAH (Old Aged Hamster)

It is **impossible** for a hamster to be six years old. Any hamster that old would be grey and wear glasses. It would have a teeny tiny walking frame and a **Stannah Stair-wheel.**

If you have a hamster that is five or six years old or if you know someone who does, I'm afraid there is only one **explanation:**

Hamster conspiracy theory: Page 222

Why have I got so many hamsters?

'Hello,' you say to the man who runs the pet shop. 'I'd like to buy some hamsters please.'

'Of course,' replies the man. 'How many would you like?'

'I'd like two please,' you say. 'But make sure that they are both girl hamsters. I don't want any babies.'

'Okay. These two are both girls.'

'Are you sure?'

'Yes.'

Feeding a pet: Page 22

You take the hamsters home, give them a **cage** and **food bowls** and all that sort of stuff. All is well. You **play** with your hamsters. You love your hamsters. You give them **names** and tell everyone about them.

But then, one of your hamsters gets **fatter...**

And then one day you notice that you have **piles of baby hamsters.**

'**W**hy have I got so many hamsters?' you ask yourself.

Well, what has happened is that the man who runs the pet shop was **wrong.** He didn't sell you two girl hamsters at all. He sold you one girl hamster and one boy hamster by **mistake.**

Now, I don't know how it happens but if you leave a girl hamster and a boy hamster together for long enough (about five minutes) they will start a **family** and soon you'll have more hamsters than you know what to do with. The only thing you can do in this situation is try and give them away to friends and relatives. I wish you **luck** with this.

Hamsters:
Page 138

Complications caused by keeping animals in the bath: Page 56

Trouble with pets: Page 54

Relocation of pets: Page 230

Holidays on the Moon

Imagine if you could go on holiday to the **Moon!** I know you can't imagine it now, but when I was your age, no one went abroad on holiday. We had to go to nearby rainy beaches made of **gravel.** Now children go all over the world on their holidays. So maybe in 20 or 30 years time, it will be possible to get on a **space rocket** and go on holiday to the Moon!

What would **you** do?

You might think that there wouldn't be very many **activities** available but rather excitingly, a few years ago a group of **Airedale Terriers** settled on the Moon and have been running a very successful business providing facilities for tourists.

Airedale
Terriers:
Page 86

You could play **Crazy Golf.**

CRAZY
GOLF

You could eat as much **cheese** as you like.

You could go fishing for **Lunar Guppies.**

Made-up types
of fish:
Page 116

Dogs and
fires:
Page 72

Made-up types of dog

Some dogs have such **ridiculous** names that they sound like someone just made them up. The **Chihuahua,** for example, is one of the most ridiculous sounding dogs of all time but it is, in fact, a **real name** for a dog.

Here are some dogs that are **entirely made-up** and do not exist at all:

The Transylvanian Nose Hound

This dog is very **useful** for tracking **vampires** and weird families of tiny animals.

The Long-Eared Trout Spotter

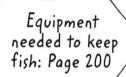

This wonderful furry **quadruped** runs along the side of rivers and then stands perfectly still when it sees a fish. (Do not get this type of dog if you own goldfish — it will be **funny** at first but then get really **boring.** People will just wonder why your dog is always pointing at the fish tank.)

The Irish Dinghy Dog

Equipment needed to keep fish: Page 200

This strange **canine** is very wide and round and can be used as a boat to cross rivers and small lakes. Some Irish Dinghy Dogs have a particularly **flat tail,** which they use as a kind of oar to propel them to speeds of up to **40 mph.**

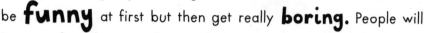

The Flat-Coated Document Retriever

This dog is about the same size as a Golden Retriever but **special pads** on the soles of its paws allow it to work touchscreen devices and **find documents** and photos which you thought you had lost but were actually hidden somewhere deep in your hard drive.

The Broader Collie

Just like a normal collie but more **difficult** to understand.

The Round-Nosed Turtle Polisher

You might think that this would be a dog with a **round nose,** which is used for **polishing** the shells of turtles. Quite disappointingly, the Round-Nosed Turtle Polisher actually has a nose the shape of a **banana** and is terrified of turtles and all animals with shells such as snails, tortoises and eggs.

The Frisbee Terrier

This is a **charming** little creature who throws itself over long distances, **catches** itself mid-air and then brings itself back to where it started. No one is quite sure what the point of this behaviour is, but it is extremely **funny** to watch.

The Nicaraguan Lobster Hound

This is an **underwater** hunting dog that can be used to gather seafood. The dog can hold its breath for over five minutes and has been trained to **sink** to the bottom of the ocean by stuffing stones in its **knickers.**

The Cumberland Sausage-Dog

This is a particularly long type of **sausage dog** which **curls** itself up into a spiral like a Cumberland Sausage.

The Wurlitzer Dumpling Dog

This dog originated in the **Austrian Alps.** Despite looking no more remarkable than a **dumpling,** it is able to sing all sorts of tunes using specially developed throat muscles. Wurlitzer

Royal Society for Made-Up Animals: Page 174

Chihuahuas: Page 88

Portmanteau dogs: Page 96

puppies are taken to Vienna to hear **opera** and **classical music.** By the time they are one year old, they have learned an entire Beethoven concerto and can impersonate most instruments in an orchestra. Wurlitzers can theoretically learn any tune but traditionally they **sing** Bach, Offenbach and Woofgang Mozart.

Being attacked by cats: Why have you got scratches on your face?

Lots of people will tell you that cats are **lovely.** Why is it then, that I'm always meeting small people with **scratches** all over their face?

Oh no. What happened to you? Did you ride your scooter into a hedge?

No. I've got a kitten.

Your kitten did that to your face?

Yes. I love him.

He doesn't love you.

If you have a **cat,** I'm sure your cat is lovely but I don't think cats actually love you. I think they just want **food.** Then again, I suppose you could say the same thing about most dogs really. My dog will only do **tricks** if there is a **biscuit** involved. I wonder which one is best: cats or dogs?

Cats V dogs:
Page 221

Pets that go bonkers:
Page 58

Tummy tickling:
Page 79

One thing that is definitely **different** between cats and dogs is what happens if you **tickle** them on the **tummy!**

Keeping goldfish in the toilet

A THRONE OF GOLD(fish)

Most people keep fish in a tank or a bowl. But many people around the world have started keeping goldfish in their toilet.

The main advantage of keeping fish in your toilet is that you don't have to buy a tank or a bowl.

One of the disadvantages of keeping fish in your toilet is that you can't go to the toilet without weeing or pooing on your fish. And fish don't like that.

But the main disadvantage of keeping fish in your toilet is that you must remember not to flush it. If you do, your fish will disappear forever!

Overall, keeping fish in your toilet is a really silly thing to do.

What on Earth are libraries?

Most towns and some villages have a **library.** They have existed for thousands of years as a place to keep books and store **knowledge.** Recently libraries have been **struggling** a bit because people tend to use the **Internet** to find out information, rather than **books.**

But being in a room that is full of books is a **marvellous** thing. Just think about how many **words** there are in a library. Each of those words has been thought of, and carefully chosen, by tens of thousands of people. That must make it a **special** place to be.

Maybe all sorts of things could happen in libraries, and be improved by being surrounded by **books.** Occasionally, you see that a library is being used for poetry workshops or **ukulele lessons.** Sometimes, they have **authors** visiting and talking about their books or storytellers telling their tales. All of these activities are much better because they are in a library.

I wonder if **badminton** would be better in a library.

Yoga would **definitely** work, as would, Yak-Decorating, Yurt Designing and Yoghurt Making.

Dressage probably wouldn't be quite as **successful.**

Lots of **schools** have libraries. If your school has a library it's probably not just a place to read books. Libraries are also **safe** places to be. They are calmer than the playground or the dinner hall. It's the books that keep things **calm.**

Libraries are also often home to **librarians.** These are strange creatures who live in a little nest between bookshelves. There is a **wonderful** thing that a librarian can do that the Internet isn't so good at: a librarian can recommend a book that you haven't thought of. Try it: go up to a librarian and say:

I've been reading this book about pets by James Campbell. What do you think I should read next?

Famous pets throughout history: Page 132

Who is Shakespeare and why should I give a cat's bum about him?: Page 142

Guinea pigs

Guinea pigs are funny little **creatures.** I have done some research and have discovered that Guinea is a country in Africa and a pig is a farm animal that is most commonly turned into **bacon.** So you would think that a guinea pig is a pig from **Africa.** But it is not. The guinea pig is not a pig and it does not originate from Guinea in Africa.

Guinea pigs are excellent pets in that they are very **friendly** and **affectionate.** They like being played with. They love being stroked and you can do all sorts of unusual things with them.

The guinea pig is a kind of rodent (which is a family that includes rats and mice) and comes from the Andes in South America.

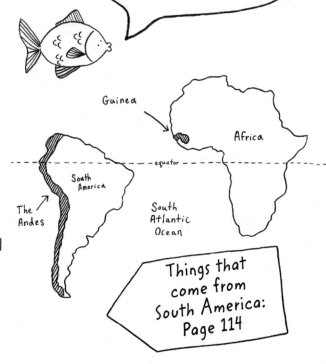

Guinea

Africa

equator

South America

The Andes

South Atlantic Ocean

Things that come from South America: Page 114

Guinea pigs are quite a bit **bigger** than hamsters and live a lot **longer.**

You might often hear people use the phrase 'guinea pig' to describe something that is being **experimented** on. This is because guinea pigs have been used by scientists for **experiments.** A lot of people think this is not a very nice thing to do to guinea pigs, or any animal. I have, however, devised a series of safe and ethical experiments that you can do with your pets, guinea pigs or otherwise.

How long do pets live?: Page 231

Safe and ethical experiments you can do with your pets: Page 40

Guinea pigs are very popular in **Peru** where they originate from but people there don't keep them as pets – they eat them! So if you have a pet guinea pig, don't take it on **holiday** to Peru!

Things you can fire with a space catapult

Once you've got yourself a **space catapult...** (And if you don't know where to get one, the company Bucheto make excellent space catapults.) You need to have a think about what you want to fire into space with it. And why.

Machines from Bucheto: Page 190

Dogs and fires: Page 72

The obvious thing to fire is **a dog** because dogs have **heatproof** noses and will survive the burn as they travel through the atmosphere at millions of miles an hour. Things that are not heatproof will not do very well at being catapulted through space. For example, if you try and send a **chocolate fudge cake** into space it will melt and disintegrate before it has even left the Earth's atmosphere.

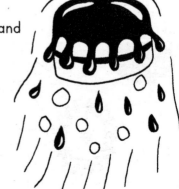

Similarly, cheese is a terrible thing to fire into space. This is mainly why all of the **cheese** on the Moon has stayed where it is. People have tried sending it to Earth but every time they fire some with their space catapult, the cheese has **melted** into sticky strings, covered everyone with it and generally made all the people involved look **stupid.**

Good things to fire into space include poisonous snakes, sharks and science teachers...

Something you must never, ever, **ever, ever** do, under any circumstances, is fire a cat into space. Just because the word **CAT** is the first part of CATapult does not mean the two things are compatible.

165

Portmanteau words

Portmanteau words are parts of two words **stuck together,** to make a new word that sounds a bit like both words. The word **'infotainment'** is a good example. It is half of 'information' and half of 'entertainment'. The word infotainment is used to describe something both **informative** and **entertaining.** A bit like this book.

Lewis Carroll invented lots of **portmanteau** words and put them in his books and poems. 'Mimsy', for example, means miserable and flimsy. 'Frumious' means **fuming** and **furious** at the same time.

Lewis Carroll (who wrote Alice in Wonderland amongst other things) was the first to use the phrase 'portmanteau words' about 150 years ago.

If you can find a copy of his **poem** The Jabberwocky, you will see lots of portmanteau words that Carroll invented. Lewis Carroll named this type of word after the **portmanteau suitcase,** which was very popular in the 19th century, and was a suitcase that had two parts to it. I would like to **invent** some **new** types of words named after bags:

Handbag Words: Words which only your Nan uses: *Beatles, Right Bobby Dazzler, Snazzy, Video, Mend* and *Pumps* (to describe trainers).

Sleeping Bag Words: Words you say when you are asleep: *Wuvoo, zzznore, aaahhhhmmmm, flunk* and *fivemoreminutes.*

School Bag Words: Words which you only use at school and will never use anywhere else: *Recorder, pencil-sharpener, geography, subjunctive, assembly* and *curriculum.*

Suitcase Words: Really big words that need to be on wheels if you want to move them anywhere: *antidisestablishmentarianism, juxtaposition* and *Floccinaucinihilipihunexpectediteminbaggingarea.*

Portmanteau dogs: Page 96

The environmental consequences of owning a pet: Page 238

Made-up types of cat: Page 216

The Airedale
Air Museum

The Airedale Air Museum contains various **artefacts** and **exhibitions** about air and is officially the most **boring** museum in the world. You might think it would be a museum about aeroplanes and helicopters but no. It's just about **AIR.**

One of the least interesting sections is the **Last Breath Room.** In various jars are the last breaths of over 1,000 famous people. It includes the **last gasps** of air of Lord Nelson, Cleopatra and a small mouldy man called Henry.

In the basement of the Airedale Air Museum is the **Trump Museum,** which contains thousands of last guffs collected in jars from over 900 people. In here, if you really want to — you can look at the **bottom-burps** of Mussolini, Joan of Arc and various fat old Labradors.

There are also some **tiny jars**, which contain the **farts** of over a dozen hamsters, gerbils and guinea pigs.

My **favourite** exhibition at the Airedale Air Museum is the one dedicated to the Airedale Terrier – the world's only **inflatable dog** – which were used to send messages across the English Channel during the **French Revolution.**

Airedale Terriers: Page 86

Illegal things you still can't do on a horse: Page 110

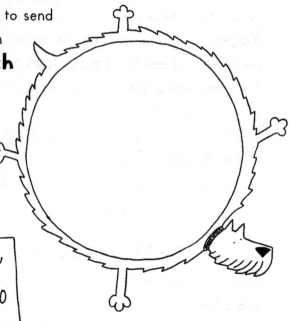

My grandparents' cat

My grandparents used to have a cat. It was a **Persian** cat.

Persians are long-haired cats and you have to brush them a lot or they get all **knotted.**

Different types of cat:
Page 124

I am **allergic** to cats and I'm sure that this cat **knew** that I was allergic to it. And it was very **pleased** about this.

I would visit my grandparents and after a while I would start to feel **poorly.** Then I would fall asleep and wake up a while later with my eyes stuck together with **eye snot** and wheezing like a broken steam train. I'd manage to get one eye open and there would be the cat, just sitting and **looking at me.**

Pets that can do jobs

Of all the pets, dogs are the most **useful** because they can **actually** do jobs. Other pets are, of course, perfectly capable of getting jobs. A cat could easily work as someone's **hat.**

Or a hamster could hook up his wheel to an **electricity generator** and power a television.

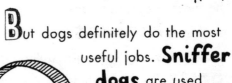

But dogs definitely do the most useful jobs. **Sniffer dogs** are used by the police and army to sniff out illegal things and **explosives.**

A dog's nose is more than a **1,000 times** more sensitive than our nose. That's why if you do a bottom burp in a dog's face it will go **cross-eyed** and fall over.

You might see dogs helping people as well. **Guide Dogs** look after blind people and **Hearing Dogs** help the deaf. Search for a video called '*14 animals with incredible jobs*' on YouTube. You'll find elephant painters, life-saving dogs and seeing miniature horses!

You'll notice that you don't get **Guide Cats.** If cats were in charge of leading blind people around the place you'd see folks walking along the tops of fences and railings. This could be seen as evidence that dogs are **better** than cats...

Cats V dogs: Page 221

The most useful pets are probably **chickens** (because you can get eggs out of them) and **worms** (because they turn things into compost).

Pets which aren't in this book much: Page 236

Great Danes: Page 108

Getting a rescue pet: Page 26

Royal Society for Made-Up Animals

In 1888, Princess Albert of Verneuil-Sur-Avre visited England because someone had told her that a herd of **Bolivian Lemurs** were living in the jungles of Norfolk. When she realised that these animals were **made-up** she was at first a bit cross, but then laughed at the joke for six hours, until a little bit of **wee** came out and she had to have a lie down.

The next morning she decided to use some of her **considerable fortune** to start the Royal Society for Made-Up Animals. Since then, the Society has catalogued all the world's animals that they couldn't find. These include:

The Austrian Lion ⟶

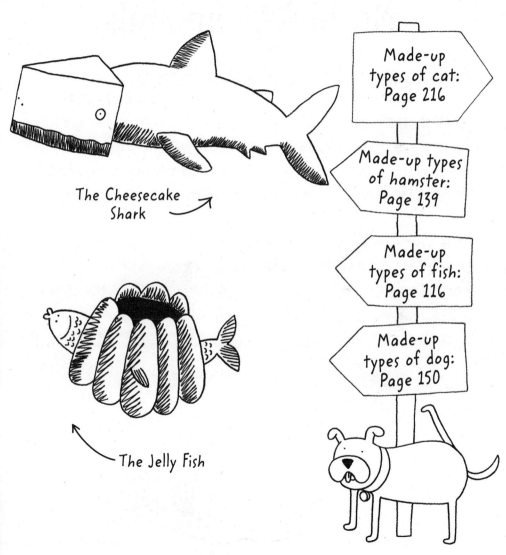

And these pets...

Made-up types of cat: Page 216

Made-up types of hamster: Page 139

Made-up types of fish: Page 116

Made-up types of dog: Page 150

The Cheesecake Shark

The Jelly Fish

People who copied their look from their dogs

Have you ever heard it said that people start to look like their pets? Here are some people who copied their whole look from their dog. Search online for dogs who look like their owners and you'll see that's **actually true!**

Famous pets throughout history: Page 132

Mrs Poodle

Harry
Husky

Mick Mastiff
the bodybuilder

Gregory
Greyhound

2

1

Ponies

The most **important** thing you have to know about ponies is that they are **really big.** A pony is probably the biggest pet anyone can have without needing special permission from the **government.**

Generally speaking there are two types of people. Some people look at a horse in a field and they think to themselves, 'Hmmm. That's a lovely animal. It is beautiful and majestic. What a wonderful creation. I'm going to leave it alone and carry on with my walk.'

Other people however, look at a horse and say to themselves, 'That is brilliant. I need to sit on it!'

You **don't** do that with other pets, do you? You don't look at a guinea pig and say, 'I'm going to sit on that guinea pig and ride it round the garden.'

You need lots of space to keep a pony. You are not allowed to keep them in your **bath.**

Complications caused by keeping animals in the bath: Page 56

Most people keep their pony in a field or pay someone who owns a field to keep it there.

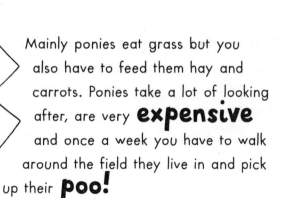

One pet bigger:
Page 14

Beginning page:
Page 9

Horse racing:
Page 184

James visits a horse show:
Page 182

Mainly ponies eat grass but you also have to feed them hay and carrots. Ponies take a lot of looking after, are very **expensive** and once a week you have to walk around the field they live in and pick up their **poo!**

I don't have much experience of ponies but I did once go to a horse show, which was **hilarious.**

Pony equipment and other tack

You can't just jump on a horse and start riding it. You need **equipment.** You need a special helmet, riding boots with a heel so they don't slip through the stirrup and a long sleeved shirt. You also need a **cape** and a **top hat.**

Your horse will need **equipment** too. This is called 'tack' and you usually get it from something called a **tack shop.**

Your horse will need a **saddle.** This is a special seat which ties around your horse's belly. This way you can sit on your horse without **falling off.** Make sure you put it on the **right way** up. If you put it on upside down you will look like this...

Ponies: Page 178

And you'll **bump your head** on the ground as you ride along.

James visits a horse show

I once went to a **horse show.** By accident really. It was a long time ago and at the time I was quite **afraid** of horses. I'd been invited to tell stories to some of the children at the show.

My main fear is the **sheer size** of horses. They are **massive** animals. When I was a child, a horse once trod on my foot and it really hurt. I'm now not afraid of horses at all. In fact, a couple of years ago I survived **wild** horses visiting my campsite...

The wild ponies of Caenlochan: Page 90

The most **terrifying** part of the horse show was when I was queuing up to get a cup of tea. I was minding my own business and talking to myself when I realised that something was breathing very **hot air** down the back of my neck. I slowly turned around to see a horse, queuing up for a cup of tea behind me. I didn't even know that horses drank tea.

I thought to myself, 'It'll be okay though. Someone **responsible** will be sitting on top of this horse.'

So I looked up and who was in charge of this **gigantic beast?** A seven-year-old girl with massive teeth!

To me, that's like realising that there is a **machine gun** behind you and then noticing that the machine gun is being looked after by a small monkey with a terrifying **grin** on his face.

Aaaaaargggghhhhh!!!!

Ponies:
Page 178

Horse racing

Horse racing is a sport where tiny **jockeys** sit on huge horses and see who can get round a field the fastest. Many people like watching horse racing. Sometimes it's **funny** too. Find a video called *'Funny Horseracing Bloopers Compilation'* and you'll see what I mean!

I prefer **horse-tracing** which is where you get a **massive sheet** of thin paper, throw it over a horse and try and draw its outline with a pencil before it gets bored and trots off to the shops. This is very difficult and only the best **horse-tracers** can manage it.

Weird sports: Page 218

184

Another sport you might be interested in is **horse-lacing**. This is where you tie horses together into a gigantic shoe. This is a ridiculous sport and only silly people do this. If you ever see someone trying to lace a horse suggest they get themselves a really **clever dog** to do their thinking for them.

When people do horse racing, they either do it over fences or on the flat. Please don't get **confused** by this. Racing on the flat is not the same as racing **in** a flat. Where would you keep a pony in a **flat?** In the **bath?**

Complications caused by keeping animals in the bath: Page 56

My pony needs new shoes

Weirdly, ponies need to wear shoes. Not shoes like your shoes but big lumps of **metal** that are curved like the shape of a...
horseshoe.

When you buy your horse, you will probably be told how old its shoes are. But usually, a horse needs a new set of shoes every six to eight weeks or so — depending on how much you've been riding it, how heavy you are and how much **dancing** your horse does.

Unfortunately you can't go to a **shoe shop** with your pony. You have to phone someone called a **farrier.** It's a farrier's job to go around the place putting new shoes on ponies. This is not something you **should try** yourself...

If you can't find a farrier, a **farry** will do. And best of all would be a **farriest.** But a farrier does the job perfectly well.

Interestingly, **wild ponies** don't wear any shoes at all. But wild ponies are really **scary.**

Trouble with pets: Page 54

The wild ponies of Caenlochan: page 90

Sausage-horsing

For this game you need to have certain things in place.

1. The first thing you need is a **responsible** grown-up.

How to test if a grown-up is responsible: Page 198

2. Next you will need some spare **cooked sausages.** One is enough. Six is better. A **bucket** full of sausages is best of all.

3. Finally you will need a horse and **permission** from the horse's owner (if it isn't your own horse) to **throw sausages** at it.

Of course. That's absolutely fine. As long as they're not Cumberland. He hates Cumberland sausages.

Is it okay if I throw sausages at your horse?

The game involves standing quite a fair distance from the horse and then throwing sausages at it until you get one to land on its back. Or the **horse leaves.**

The **world record** for sausage-horsing is held by Loughborough Picket who successfully threw **87 sausages** onto the back of his horse. World record officials said that he could have done more but unfortunately the field was invaded by a load of sausage dogs who were **protesting** against the sport. Loughborough Picket was not fazed by this at all but simply started **throwing sausage dogs** at the horse instead.

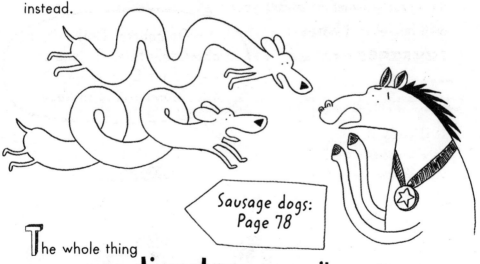

Sausage dogs:
Page 78

The whole thing was a complete **disaster** and I **can't recommend** doing this at all.

Machines from Bucheto

Bucheto is my new favourite company. They are based in **Argentina** and they make the most amazing machines, including the following:

Space Catapults

Things you can fire with a space catapult: Page 164

These are **giant** devices that have the power to **catapult** pretty much anything into outer space. I'm not sure how they do it but, according to their website, they use the elastic from a huge pair of **granny knickers.**

Hydraulic Guinea Pig Launcher

You can only buy one of these if you have a **license** and are a properly **trained** guinea pig handler. This device is used to **hurl guinea pigs** (safely) across huge distances. It comes with little parachute packs for the guinea pig to wear so that it lands **gently.**

Polar Bear Repelling Machine

If you live in a place with lots of **polar bears** (like the Arctic or some parts of Scotland) you might want one of these. It's about the size of a **pineapple** and sits on your bedside table, sending out sonic beams that polar bears can't stand. I've got one and I have never been **troubled** by polar bears.

Automatic Shaver, Nit-Vacuum and Head Painter

If you have nits, this machine is **awesome.** It's slightly bigger than a child's head and all you do is wear it like a **mechanical hat.** The machine detects the presence of nits and then uses whirling razor blades to remove all of your hair. A vacuum nozzle then **sucks the nits** off your scalp and then a dozen tiny paintbrushes paint your head with varnish, creating a seal that prevents nits from ever coming back.

Dogs and fires: Page 72

What to do if you find a pet at the bottom of your bed: Page 61

Pet allergies

Allergies can be a **nightmare.** Some people are allergic to **pollen,** dust and even some foods. But what about pet allergies? How can anyone be allergic to a **cute,** fluffy creature?

We all have **immune** systems that protect us from poisonous and dangerous stuff, like **smoke.** If you're sitting next to a campfire and the smoke gets in your face and your mouth, your body will start doing things to protect you from the smoke. You'll start **coughing** and **wheezing** to get it out of your lungs and your eyes will start watering to flush the smoke particles out before they get into your head and your brain. This is all perfectly **normal.**

How to make a campfire: Page 140

People with pet allergies have an oversensitive immune system which is triggered by harmless things like cats or dogs. Most people who are allergic to pets are actually allergic to the dust on the fur (which is called dander), the saliva of the animal or its urine! All these things get on the pet's fur and then float around in the air of your house.

Portmanteau dogs: Page 96

If someone has a **pet allergy**, there isn't a lot they can do about it apart from avoiding the thing they are allergic to. I am allergic to cats so I just try and **stay away** from them.

Problems come though, if you get a pet and then discover that someone in your family is allergic to it... someone who didn't know they were **allergic** until now.

The main thing with pet allergies is that people who don't have pet allergies find it very difficult to understand what the **problem** is. If I go to someone's house and they have a cat, I tell them that I am allergic and all they do is open a window.

I often wonder what it would be like if cats were allergic to **me.** Imagine if I went round my friend's house and their cat started sneezing and wheezing.

I'm terribly sorry but I think my cat is allergic to you. Please leave.

Someone in your house is allergic to your pet: Page 235

193

A funny story about litter trays

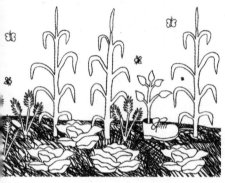

A long time ago my allotment neighbour invited me and my son (who was about five) to her family's house for **Sunday lunch.**

That Sunday, I took my son to their very nice house, which was a converted **school house.** We'll call my son Joe — because that's his name. Joe was very pleased to find that when they converted the house they put a **slide** in next to the stairs. They had lots of children and the idea was that the children would slide down in the morning and that would make a **great start** to anyone's day.

Litter trays:
Page 28

Poo identification table: Page 34

We had lunch and then the children ran around playing. At one point, one of the grown-ups said, 'Isn't it nice when there are lots of children together?' Everyone agreed but I felt a **terrible feeling** in my tummy. I knew something was wrong.

'I'm just going to check on Joe,' I said and went for a wander around the house. It didn't take long to find my son. He had **NOT** been playing with the other children. No. Instead, he had gone upstairs and found a cat's **litter tray.** He had then taken out the contents of the litter tray (cat litter and dried up pieces of poo) and had spent a long time **firing** it down the slide. By the time I discovered this, he had covered the hallway in cat litter and **poo.**

We didn't become **friends** with that family for some reason.

Goldfish

I like **goldfish.** In many ways they are a really simple pet. You don't have to take them for walks. They don't have to be **groomed.** And if they **die,** you can usually get another one that looks exactly the same and pretend it's the same one.

On the other hand, you can't teach goldfish any **tricks.** You can't **cuddle** them and you have to create a whole environment for them to live in.

Personally, I think the **best environment** for keeping a fish is salt, vinegar, batter and in my tummy. But apparently this does not count as looking after it.

How to prove you know how to look after a fish: Page 204

Hamster conspiracy theory: Page 222

Keeping goldfish in the toilet: Page 158

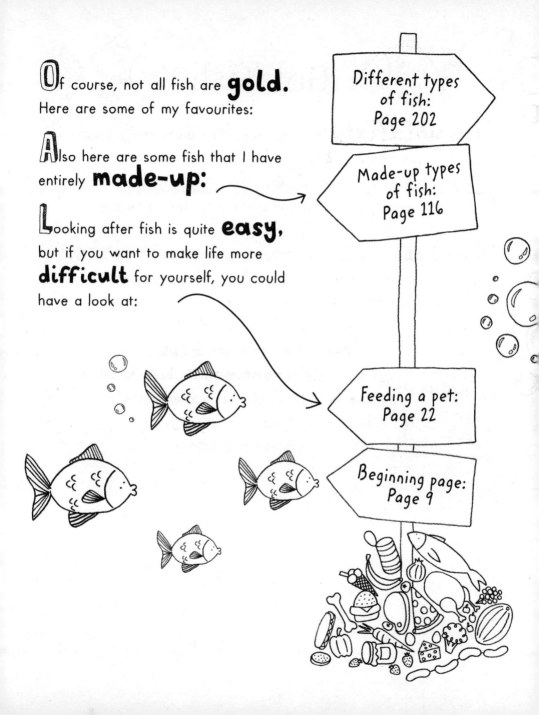

Of course, not all fish are **gold.** Here are some of my favourites:

Also here are some fish that I have entirely **made-up:**

Looking after fish is quite **easy,** but if you want to make life more **difficult** for yourself, you could have a look at:

Different types of fish: Page 202

Made-up types of fish: Page 116

Feeding a pet: Page 22

Beginning page: Page 9

How to test if a grown-up is responsible

There are many **occasions** in this book where I suggest that you do something with a **responsible adult.** In fact, there are all sorts of other books and television programmes and **whatnots** where people say, 'And remember to always do this with the help of a responsible adult.'

But how do you know if an **adult** is responsible or not? If you want to use a massive pair of **sharp scissors** to cut the top off a bottle of washing-up liquid? Which grown-up do you choose to help you?

Do you ask Mad Uncle Basil who thinks he is a walrus? **No.**

Do you ask your **neighbour** who collects broken cars and makes piles of them in his front garden? **Definitely not.**

Do you ask Mrs Cloud who is a teaching assistant at your school and seems to be responsible but is wearing her shoes on the wrong feet? **Possibly.**

But then again, all those people might actually be really **sensible** and **responsible.** It's difficult to tell. So, here is my test to find out if a grown-up is responsible **or not.**

Sit them down and **calmly** ask them this question:

You know how by the time I'm your age there are going to be about nine billion people living on this planet and we will have run out of oil and coal and gas? What are you personally doing to make sure me and my children will have renewable forms of energy and clean water to drink?

The environmental consequences of owning a pet: Page 238

If they don't have a **decent** answer to this then they are **not** a responsible grown-up and you shouldn't ask them to help you with anything.

Equipment needed to keep fish

If you are keeping fish you need to provide their entire environment, otherwise they will **die.** Some fish like living in cold water, others prefer warm water. You also need to use a **filter system** to take out their **poo** and a light to show them what's going on. You will definitely need a tank to keep them in (an old welly boot will not do the job) and it will probably need to be near a plug socket because keeping fish requires **electricity...**

The environmental consequences of owning a pet: Page 238

Unless you are keeping **electric eels.** Electric eels will power themselves and anything that touches them.

If you're **serious** about going to get a fish it's really important that you ask the advice of a real person. Reading a book about it or going online is not the answer. Go to a **fish shop** and ask a person.

(When I say a fish shop, I don't mean a fish and chip shop. People in a fish and chip shop probably don't know how to keep fish alive.)

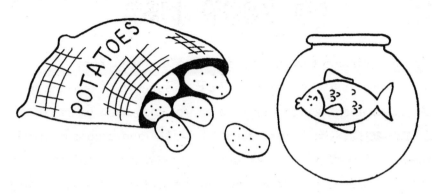

Go to a shop that sells **pet fish!** Whatever you do, don't do what I did with my pet fish when I was little...

My goldfish: Page 205

Portmanteau dogs: Page 96

Different types of fish

Here are some of my **favourites:**

Guppy

These fish are **beautiful** and have a stupid name. What more could you want from a fish?

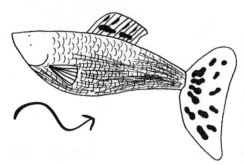

Suckermouth Catfish

These fish are really **ugly** and sound **disgusting.**

Black Molly

This is a very **peaceful** fish.
Which is what you want from a fish
really. You don't want an angry fish.
No one wants an **angry** fish.

Carp

There are many different types of carp. **Mirror Carp**
are the most lovely looking but you wouldn't want to keep them in
a tank because they are **massive.**

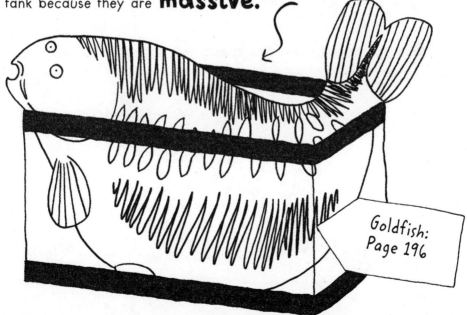

Goldfish:
Page 196

How to prove you know how to look after a fish

You can't just walk into a **aquarium** and say, 'Hey. Give me some fish!' They won't sell you any fish unless you can show that you know what you're doing.

First you need to fill your tank with water and let it settle. If you put fish into water that has come straight out of the tap, the **chlorine** and other nasty things that we put in our tap water will **kill** your fish or even worse, turn them into **mutant** fish that will take over the world!

Once you've left your tank **humming** and **filtering** for a week or so, take a bottle full of the water to your fish-selling shop. They will **test** it and then, if you have done everything correctly, you will have everything necessary to look after fish. **Hooray!**

Your pet dies: Page 233

Goldfish: Page 196

My goldfish

When I was a small child I lived with my grandparents for a while in a **higgledy piggledy** half-house, half-restaurant. Our front door opened out onto the market square and once a year, the fair would come to town and plonk itself right outside our door. Every time the **fair** would come, we would get a goldfish in a plastic bag and some **candy-floss.** The candy-floss would usually last the longest!

This was possibly because of the way we kept the fish. We had a **goldfish bowl** which we filled with cold water. Within a couple of weeks, the goldfish would start to struggle. Eventually the goldfish would die and I would have to flush it down the **toilet.**

This is not the way to look after a goldfish. If you want to know how to look after a goldfish, go to a shop that sells them and ask a **real person.** Whatever you do, **don't ask me.**

Equipment needed to keep fish: Page 200

205

Dogs that are named after food

The great thing about **dogs** is that there are so many **breeds.** Lots of dogs have very **silly names.** Some sound a bit **rude.** Some sound really complicated. Some, however, sound like they have been named after food. The most obvious one is the **sausage dog.** The sausage dog is called the sausage dog because it is in the shape of a sausage. Apparently our **American** friends call sausage dogs 'Wieners', because that is what they call sausages.

Sausage dogs:
Page 78

Other dogs that are named after food include:

The Border
Cauliflower

The English Mustard Spaniel

The Rhodesian Fridgeback

Jack Russell sprouts are not just for Christmas: Page 215

The Jack Russell Sprout

The Smoked Salmon And Cream-Cheese Beagle

Vehicles for pets

Most pets are perfectly **happy** walking or swimming or scuttling around in a normal way. But why not make things more **fun** for them? Here are some **vehicles** you can get for your pets.

Motorbikes

MOTORBIKES FOR DOGS are an excellent **invention.** They are just the right size for a small dog to climb on and rev up. That way they can **chase cars,** each other and enter motorcycle races!

Machines from Bucheto:
Page 190

Small dogs versus big dogs:
Page 94

Space Rockets

SPACE ROCKETS FOR CATS are one of my **favourites**. These are relatively small space rockets that you can launch from a **dustbin** in your back garden and give your cat an experience of a **lifetime**.

Mobile tanks

MOBILE TANKS FOR FISH are truly **wonderful.** The whole tank is placed on wheels and when the fish moves towards one side of the tank or other, special **sensors** tell the computer which way to move the wheels. This way the fish can steer itself all over the place and go on **adventures.**

My fish are dead

Sorry about that. You probably fed them too much or not enough. Or the **wrong thing.** Or maybe one of them ate all the other fish and then **exploded.**

When my fish died I did wonder if I should **flush** my fish down the **toilet** like a **shimmery poo,** so he could go out to sea and join his fishy friends. This would've been a bad idea. Whatever has happened, get a **grown-up** to sort things out.

It's okay to feel **sad** about dead fish. In fact, it's okay to feel anything about anything really. If it helps, you might be interested to learn about **reincarnation.** Some people – and I'm one of them – believe that when things die they come back again as **something else.**

Trouble with pets: Page 54

Record-breaking pets

Sometimes real life is better than **fiction.** If you go to the website of The Guinness Book Of World Records you will find thousands of **record-breaking** pets. My favourite is the record for most **balloons popped** by a dog in a minute.

If my dog attempted this record it would probably only pop one balloon and then run away **crying.**

Do you think your pet could be a **record breaker?** There must be something it's really **good** at. Maybe your hamster is excellent at playing **Connect 4?**

Playing Connect 4 with your pet: Page 50

You can also search on YouTube for '*10 Amazing Animal World Records*'. There are some hilarious animals that made the list!

Tummy tickling: Page 79

What on Earth is Latin and why should I give a hamster poo about it?

Latin is a language spoken in **ancient Rome** about 3,000 years ago. It was originally spoken by the people of **Latium** but it spread to become the language of the Roman Empire.

What has this got to do with **me?** I hear you ask.

Well, **interestingly**, even though no one really speaks **Latin** any more, lots of our modern languages like Italian and Spanish have a lot of Latin in them. Even **English** has lots of words that are either Latin or come from Latin.

Antenna, bonus, digital, formula and *posterior* are all Latin words.

In some schools, children have to **learn** Latin even though you can't really speak it anywhere. Children all over the world say the rhyme:

> Latin is a dead language
> As dead as dead can be.
> It killed off all the Romans
> And now it's killing me.

Learning Latin may indeed be extremely **painful** but there is no evidence that it is **dangerous** or might kill you.

Cats:
Page 118

Hamsters:
Page 138

More about nits

There is a **creature** which is not a pet but which sometimes lives in your hair without paying any rent. These creatures are sometimes called **nits** or **head lice.** Mostly, however, they are called...

'Aaahhh, get them out of my hair!'

There are **three** main ways of getting rid of nits:

1. You can use a special **nit comb.** One of your grown-ups grabs you in some sort of **wrestling** hold, while another scrapes a piece of metal over your scalp, until your screaming scares the nits and they run away.

2. Alternatively you can use Anti-Nit Shampoo. This is like **poison** for nits. They think they are being washed but really they are being exterminated.

3. The third way to get rid of nits is to **shave** all your hair off and then suck them up with a **vacuum cleaner!**

Hamsters:
Page 138

Machines
from Bucheto:
Page 190

Jack Russell Sprouts are not just for Christmas

Most pages in this book are **funny** in some way. Some pages of this book, however, are actually **serious.** This is one of them.

Every Christmas, people think it would be a good idea to buy a **Jack Russell Sprout.** They are cute, small, green and have Christmas decorations all over them. What's not to like? What these people don't realise is that Jack Russell Sprouts don't stay **small and cute.** Within six months, they will have grown into a full sized Jack Russell Cabbage.

Dogs that are named after food: Page 206

These **monstrous** creatures can grow to the size of a house. If you are tempted to buy a Jack Russell Sprout as a Christmas present then please remember that it is a lifelong **commitment** and you will need a giant shed to keep it in.

Made-up types of cat

Royal Society for Made-Up Animals: Page 174

According to the Royal Society for Made-Up Animals, there are approximately **4,000** made-up types of cat, most of them living in the UK.

The Badger Cat

This type of cat looks exactly like a **badger.** It has the same striped face and it is the same size and shape as a badger. In fact, a lot of people reckon it's just a badger.

The Smitten

The name of this cat is a **portmanteau** word derived from the phrase, 'smart kitten'. The Smitten is a cutting edge, technological cat which you can plug into your digital devices.

The best thing about the **Smitten** is that you can leave it at home while you're at school but then use your **phone** to watch it, talk to it and do **experiments** on it!

Safe and ethical experiments you can do with your pets: Page 40

Portmanteau words: Page 166

The Andalusian Sponge Cat

This weird **feline** is extremely **absorbent** and has the unfortunate habit of soaking up any liquid it goes near. People who own Andalusian Sponge Cats have to pick them up and wring them out over a drain three times a day or their furniture will be **ruined.**

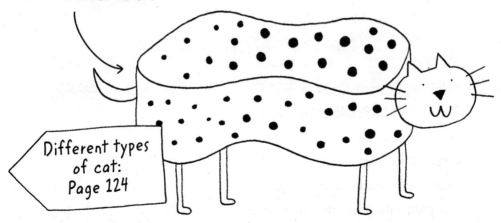

Different types of cat: Page 124

Weird sports

Avocado Throwing is a particularly **silly** sport practised by the people of Mexico. Every year, people get together and see who can throw an **avocado** the furthest. The world record is four miles.

Tortilla Boats is where people make boats out of **potato omelettes** and see how far they can sail in them before they sink. The record is California.

Horse-Tracing is a **sport** in which you put tracing paper over a horse and make a picture of it. It is a **stupid** sport and no one should do it but it is very popular in Spain.

Bopping Chihuahuas on the Head with Chipolatas is a tiny version of Bopping Dogs On The Head With Sausages. Thousands of people watch these events from a long way away with **binoculars** because they are too scared to get any closer.

Machines from Bucheto: Page 190

Cheese Rolling is a very silly activity in which people roll cheeses down a hill and then **chase** after them. I'm not sure if the **winner** is the one who catches their own cheese or if it's actually a race **AGAINST** your cheese.

Kaninhop was developed in **Sweden.** This is where they train rabbits to jump over little fences. It's **adorable.** Go and look online for videos. I promise you won't do anything else with the rest of your day.

Poohadors is a bit like **bull-fighting** but mainly involves a person in a fancy costume standing in the middle of a ring while people throw **poo** at them. Often they use a Hydraulic Guinea Pig Launcher to throw the poos at a greater velocity. You can buy these machines from **Bucheto.**

Portmanteau dogs: Page 96

Bopping dogs on the head with sausages: Page 100

Things that pets have destroyed

Once I had a shirt and a pair of **trousers** in the back of my car. My dog did a **poo** on them. I never wore that shirt and trousers again. I don't have many **rules** in life but one of them is: if something has had poo on it, throw it away. Even if it has been in the washing machine and it looks clean, it will always be the **poo shirt.**

Once I was in a school and I asked some children what was the **naughtiest** thing their pets had ever done. One boy said that his dog ate his favourite pair of **pants.** I said, 'You have a favourite pair of pants?' He said, 'No. My dog **ate them.'**

All dogs are descended from wolves: Page 106

Labradors: Page 83

Portmanteau dogs: Page 96

Cats V dogs

Over the years, I have asked **thousands** of children, which are better – cats or dogs? It seems that most people are **cat people** or **dog people.** Let's look at some of the **differences** between dogs and cats.

If you don't feed a dog, it will follow you around telling you that it loves you. If you don't feed a cat it will just go somewhere else.

If you **tickle** a dog's tummy it will love it. If you tickle a cat's tummy, **terrible** things will happen.

Dogs can do **jobs.** Cats either can't do jobs or can't be bothered.

But I suppose it doesn't matter about any of these things. If you love cats they will be your **favourites.** If you love dogs then you will think they are better.

Tummy tickling: Page 79

Being attacked by cats: why have you got scratches on your face?: Page 156

Pets that can do jobs: Page 172

Which-Pet-Flow-Chart: Page 18

Hamster conspiracy theory

As I'm sure you know, hamsters are quite **famous** for not living very long. When I talk to children, however, I'm always hearing about hamsters that have lasted **FIVE years** or sometimes even **SIX.** How is this possible, I ask myself? Are these ancient hamsters grey-coloured with glasses and walking sticks?

Life expectancy of hamsters: Page 144

There is only one **answer** as far as I am concerned and that is... The Hamster Conspiracy Theory!

Imagine you are three years old. You have pet hamster. It lives in a cage in the **utility room.** It is brown with white spots and you love it. It is probably called Mr Sprinkles.

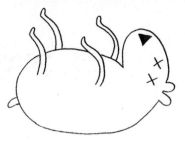

One morning, your mum notices that the hamster is unusually **quiet.** It is not spinning around in its wheel. It is **DEAD.** What is she going to do? She can't tell you that the hamster is dead. You're only **three years old.** She will have to **pretend** that everything is still okay.

That day you go to nursery and while you're playing with sand and poking other small children in the face with **yoghurty fingers,** your mum goes to the pet shop and buys a hamster which looks really similar to Mr Sprinkles. When you get home from nursery, you look in your hamster cage and say...

You: Something is different about the hamster.
Mum: No there isn't.
You: Yes there is. His spots are bigger.
Mum: No. That is Mr Sprinkles.

Brilliant names for all sorts of pets: Page 130

And so you **accept** that this new hamster is the same hamster you had before but really it is an **impostor!** Using this method, your mum can replace three or four hamsters and make you think you've had yours for seven years or more! It's a conspiracy and something needs to be done about it!

Imaginary pets

An **imaginary** pet is one that you have made-up in your head. Possible Imaginary Pets include imaginary dogs, cats, goldfish. The **advantage** of these is that people will believe you when you say you have a dog and then will be very amused when you explain that it is imaginary. Impossible Imaginary Pets include unicorns, dragons, dinosaurs, flobberly wobbly pumpkin-birds, yetis, mermaids, vampires, abominable snowmen, dodos or anything you can imagine.

Possible Imaginary Pets: Page 226

Impossible Imaginary Pets: Page 227

Any game that you can play with a **real** pet, you can play with an **imaginary** pet. But you might have to do some of the work. For example, throwing a stick for an imaginary unicorn is fun but does require you to fetch the stick yourself.

I once played a game of **20 questions** with my imaginary pet dinosaur and he was brilliant. He was able to guess my **famous** person almost immediately. It was like he was inside my mind.

The vets

Vets are brilliant. As soon as you get a pet, find a vet and **register** your pet with them. If your pet is **poorly** or needs a check up, these wonderful people are the ones to go to.

What is particularly **brilliant** about vets is that they work out what is wrong with your pet without being able to ask it any questions. It would be a lot easier if your pet could just tell you what was **wrong...**

My dog has worms: Page 64

James' sick pet story: Page 120

I've got this terrible pain in my shoulder.

The word vet is short for veterinary physician. It's basically someone who is a doctor for animals.

My pet is sick: Page 68

Possible imaginary pets

A possible imaginary pet is an imaginary version of a real pet. And they have certain **advantages.** No one is allergic to an imaginary cat.

Pet allergies: Page 192

Imaginary hamsters **don't** spin their wheel in the middle of the night and keep everyone awake. Imaginary goldfish can live in an imaginary tank the size of your **bedroom,** full of the most amazing castles and sunken spaceships. Better still, you can dive into the imaginary tank and swim with them like a **mermaid.**

Not only can imaginary ponies be ridden to school, you can ride them through the school too! Right through the assembly hall and into your classroom where they can be **parked** right in the middle of the **carpet area.**

Impossible imaginary pets

Some people say to themselves, 'If I'm going to have an imaginary pet, what's **the point** of having an imaginary version of a pet that anyone else could have? I should get a pet that is not only imaginary but also **IMPOSSIBLE!**

I spoke to a class of children in a school about their imaginary pets and it turned out that seven of them were the **proud** owners of **rainbow unicorns.** Here, however, are some even **rarer** pets.

Norfolk Lemurs

Big-eyed monkey-looking things that live in the **jungles** of the North Norfolk Coast. They like to eat fish and chips, which they **steal** from holiday-makers.

South American Dragons

Huge beasts that will **breathe fire** on anyone you don't get on with but also need to be fed twenty hundred avocados a day! And they might accidentally eat other people's **chihuahuas.**

Things that come from South America: Page 114

Envelope Sharks

These are **huge** sharks you can sit on. Not only can you ride them in or out of the water, if you give them an address they will take you to **anywhere** in the whole wide world!

Magic Hamsters

These are **microscopic** hamsters that live in yoghurt. If you use them wisely, they will help you make your own **yoghurt.**

Relocation of pets

No matter what sort of pet you have, eventually, they are going to go **somewhere else.** There are many ways that a pet's time with you can come to an end and all of them are quite **difficult** to deal with.

Here are some of the ways that your pet **relationship** can end. I've done my best to help you with whatever has happened – or **might happen.**

Beginning page:
Page 9

Your pet dies:
Page 233

Someone in your house is allergic to your pet: Page 235

Circumstances change in your house making it impossible to keep your pet: Page 234

You lose your pet: Page 232

How long do pets live?

The thing with all pets is that you never know how long they are going to live. The most difficult ones to judge are, of course, **Imaginary Pets** who will live for as long as you still believe in them.

	An indoor cat will live between 12 and 18 years. If it's an outdoor cat though, it will probably only live for 4 or 5 years because it is more likely to get an illness if it's running across roads and going through dustbins.
	The life span of a dog depends on the breed. Massive dogs only live for about 6 or 7 years, but smaller dogs can live about 14 years, which is geriatric for a dog.
	The longest living pet you could have is a giant tortoise. They can live for about 150 years. That's quite a commitment.
	Horses can live for 40 years, which is an awful long time if you think about it.
	Hamsters are the pets that will live the shortest amount of time.
	Guinea pigs will usually last a good 8 years, which is longer than a big dog.

You lose your pet

Losing your pet is an absolute **disaster.** It's terrible. One moment your pet is with you and then, suddenly, no one can find it. This is one of those **occasions** when the grown-ups have to take charge but what can you do to help?

The first thing to do is make a **poster.** Put these posters up around where you live and hope that either someone finds your pet and then knows who to phone, or your pet sees the poster and **phones home.**

Often cats can get **stuck** in places so you might want to start searching around the area and ask people to check their **sheds** and **cupboards.** I bet you a million pounds that your pet will turn up but if it doesn't, eventually you might have to accept that they are not coming back...

Your pet dies:
Page 233

Your pet dies

Your pet has **died.** Or maybe it hasn't. Maybe you've just stumbled on this page by accident or maybe you just thought you'd follow the **signpost** and see what happens.

I hope your pet has not died because when a pet dies it is **horrible.** There's absolutely no way around it. It's always going to be really **upsetting.** The fact is that pets just don't live very long.

When your pet dies things will be very **difficult** for a few days. Just let your grown-ups be in charge and help you through this. Maybe you could have a **funeral** for your pet and take it in turns to say good things about what they did. And tell the **spirit** of your beloved animal that it's okay that they have died now. They are free to float away and enjoy whatever the next part of their journey might be.

How long do pets live?: Page 231

Made-up types of hamster: Page 139

Keeping goldfish in the toilet: Page 158

You lose your pet: Page 232

Relocation of pets: Page 230

Circumstances change making it impossible to keep your pet

Maybe you were living in the **countryside** but now you are moving to an apartment in a city. Where are you going to keep the **hippo?** In the bath? Or maybe your parents are getting divorced and will be living in separate houses.

All sorts of things can happen that might mean you can't have a pet for a while. The best thing is to make sure that your pets are **happy.** They need to live somewhere suitable with people who will love them. You could **step up** to some responsibility around your pet and say, 'I will be in charge of walking the dog, polishing the cat, feeding the fish and cleaning out the hamster cage.'

Maybe that will help in the decision-making. Maybe it won't. Grown-ups are weird. Whatever happens – **good luck!** You can always get an Imaginary Pet if necessary.

Complications caused by keeping animals in the bath: Page 56

Imaginary Pets: Page 224

Relocation of pets: Page 230

Someone in your house is allergic to your pet

Imagine this: your family get a **sausage dog.** Everything is fine until you start to notice that Dad is getting really poorly. He's wheezing and sneezing and getting **grumpier** about it. Dad then finds out he is **allergic** to dogs! What can you do?

If you don't do anything about it, Dad will just get more and **more ill.**

I think the best thing is to find a friend or relative who lives close by and **guilt trip** them into having your pet. Those who are not allergic to it can then go and visit, and the member of your family who is allergic can **breathe** properly. And then, of course, the next thing to do is get a pet that no one in your house is allergic to! Fish are a safe bet.

Pet allergies: Page 192

Sausage dogs: Page 78

Brilliant names for all sorts of pets: Page 130

Relocation of pets: Page 230

Pets which aren't in this book much

This book doesn't cover *every* single pet. If it did it would be too **heavy** to lift. Here are some of the pets that aren't in this book much...

Chickens are **excellent** pets if you have a garden. One day I will write a book called *The Funny Life of The End Of The World*. I will talk properly about chickens in that.

Tortoises are **amazing** and you should really search for funny tortoise compilations on YouTube for some good laughs. Also, have you ever heard of glowing sea turtles? Look for them online — they are real **glow-in-the-dark** animals!

Worms can live in a box in your shed and you can feed them your leftover food, which they will turn into **compost** for you to grow more food in. This too will be covered in greater depth in *The Funny Life of The End Of The World*.

Aardvarks aren't even pets. They are **wild animals.** One day I will write a book called something like *The Funny Life of Wild Animals.* I will thoroughly cover aardvarks in that.

Rabbits aren't in this book much. **Lots** of people have them though. According to the Internet, there are about **1,200,000** pet rabbits in the UK alone. So I guess that about 1,200,000 people own a rabbit. Or maybe 600,000 people each own a pair of rabbits. Or maybe one person somewhere owns 1,200,000 rabbits!

Rabbits can be really **funny** too! Have a look at some funny rabbits compilation videos on YouTube.

The environmental consequences of owning a pet

We use a lot of oil in the world in petrol, heating and to make **electricity**. We even use it to make things like **bags** and packaging. Scientists reckon that by the time we get to the year 2050 we will have completely run out of oil. Are some pets **better or worse** for the environment?

Apparently, owning a large dog like a Labradoodle has the same environmental impact as owning and driving a large four wheel drive car like a Range Rover. This is because of all the meat they eat. Farm animals need a lot of land to grow in and most importantly, we also need a huge amount of land to grow rice and grain for the farm animals to eat.

There are lots of books that help you learn how to live in a more **environmentally conscious** way. If you're about to choose a pet though, and you want it to be as green as possible, then bear in mind that the more meat your pet eats, the **worse** for the planet it is.

Things that shouldn't be in this book

This book is full of things that have got **absolutely nothing** to do with pets and really shouldn't be in this book...

Susan Spot-Weld rode **naked** through the streets of Bingley in 1974 on a bicycle. If she had ridden on a pony or even a Great Dane it would have been fine but no – it was a **bicycle.**

Illegal things you still can't do on a horse: Page 110

The Toronto Maple Leaf Ice Hockey Team has nothing to do with pets. They are very **successful** Canadian athletes and should be in a book about ice hockey – not pets!

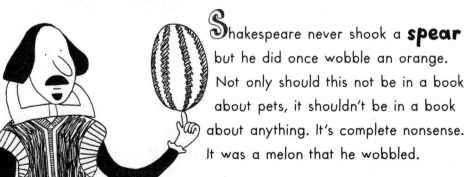

Shakespeare never shook a **spear** but he did once wobble an orange. Not only should this not be in a book about pets, it shouldn't be in a book about anything. It's complete nonsense. It was a melon that he wobbled.

The last page of the book

This is the **last** page of the book. Well done for finding it. You get to see a picture of a **naked hamster.**

Why not go back to the first page and start again? You might have missed something **terribly unimportant.**

Beginning page: Page 9